Dark Interiors

Dark Interiors

Essays on Caste and Dalit Culture

Raj Gauthaman

Translated by S. Theodore Baskaran

SAGE | *Samya*

Los Angeles | London | New Delhi
Singapore | Washington DC | Melbourne

First published in 2021 by

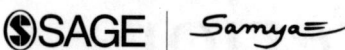

SAGE Publications India Pvt Ltd
B1/I-1 Mohan Cooperative Industrial Area
Mathura Road, New Delhi 110 044, India
www.sagepub.in

Samya
16 Southern Avenue
Kolkata 700026
www.stree-samyabooks.com

SAGE Publications Inc
2455 Teller Road
Thousand Oaks, California 91320, USA

SAGE Publications Ltd
1 Oliver's Yard, 55 City Road
London EC1Y 1SP, United Kingdom

SAGE Publications Asia-Pacific Pte Ltd
18 Cross Street #10-10/11/12
China Square Central
Singapore 048423

Published by Vivek Mehra for SAGE Publications India Pvt. Ltd. Typeset in 11/13 pt Baskerville SSi by Fidus Design Pvt. Ltd, Chandigarh.

Achuthan Kudallur (b. 1945) is one of India's foremost abstract painters. The book cover, from one of his paintings, is reproduced by courtesy.

Library of Congress Control Number: 2020949450

ISBN: 978-93-81345-63-4 (HB)

SAGE Samya team: Aritra Paul, Amrita Dutta and Neena Ganjoo
Cover Design: Swarna Jana

To
The memory of
Iyothee Thass Pandithar

Thank you for choosing a SAGE product!
If you have any comment, observation or feedback,
I would like to personally hear from you.

Please write to me at **contactceo@sagepub.in**

Vivek Mehra, Managing Director and CEO, SAGE India.

Contents

Preface

THE NINE ESSAYS on Dalit Studies that feature in this collection were written between 1991 and 2002. The first essay 'The Dalits of Tamil Nadu and Dalit Literature' (1991) is an expression of the new alertness among the dalits in India and particularly in Tamil Nadu following the centenary celebrations of Ambedkar. This essay, the first to be written in Tamil with a dalit consciousness, was brought out as a monograph by the Madurai-based Institute of Development Education, Action and Studies (IDEAS). In addition to a brief view of Tamil literature from the dalit perspective, an overview of the contemporary dalit novel, short story, play and songs is also presented. The underlying principles of the protest aesthetics of dalit literature, language, discourse are introduced. Even as dalit literature grows fast, in addition to Tamil literature as a whole getting a fillip, dalit literary principles also become complete.

Though this publication was priced at only ₹2, there were readers who would borrow it to read it. Radical Communist ideologues and structuralist highbrows ridiculed it, but the essay was well received by dalit thinkers and students. Spurred by this encouragement, I wrote with passion three essays which came out in book form: *Dalit Panpadu* in 1993.[1]

Two essays from this book 'Dalit Culture' and '*Periyapuranam*: Hierarchy and Inversion' find place in this collection (Essays 2 and 3). In addition to the ideas of Ambedkar, Self-Respect thoughts of Periyar have also aided in bringing about a new awareness. Marxist social research has also helped the process. The Dalit movement emerging

with all these ideological backings has taken a position
against Hindu fanaticism and Hindu fascism which have
assumed a fierce form in India. Only the Dalit movement has
the inherent strength, right and historical responsibility to
fight Hindu fascism.

In these two essays devices to be used in the cultural
struggle of dalits are discussed. This is just a beginning. These
devices have already been discussed by Periyar keeping the
shudras in focus. Moreover in these essays feminist ideology
is cited for comparison. The dalit struggle is connected with
the Feminist movement. Except women and dalits, I do not
think there is anyone who is discriminated at birth.

There are many dalit groups active in Tamil Nadu today.
Dalit literature has sprung and is growing. The alternative
cultural expressions of the dalits, in spheres such as politics,
art and literature have come up. This has started a discourse
in many quarters. It was in this background that the essay
'Dalit Culture' was written. It was read at the Dalit Culture
Conference in Puducherry on 7 April 1993, and deals with
the alternative culture for dalits and argues that it would
first take shape as protest culture. The approach of Periyar
to these issues was helpful in writing this essay. For dalit
discourse the writings of Periyar are a major resource.

The third essay looks from the dalit perspective at
Periyapuranam, the Saivite Tamil work, which appeared in
Tamil during the medieval era. Dalits cannot discuss the
present day situation without going into the past. The cadaver
has to be exhumed and subjected to post-mortem. The
crimes that have been concealed have to be exposed. Such a
work is undertaken in the essay on *Periyapuranam.* There are
two concepts here: Inversion and Reversion. Inversion is a
device to be used by the people to protest against hegemony.
When hegemonic powers permit the oppressed to violate
the norms for the time being and bring them back into
submission that will be reversion. Dalits should distinguish
between Inversion of the oppressed and the Reversion of the
hegemonic powers.

'Brahmins, Vellalas and the Tamil Country' (Essay 4), that was carried in 1992 in the journal *Nirapirigai*, put out from Puducherry, attempts to examine how after the fifteenth century, the traditional hegemonic castes, Telugu brahmins and vellala landowning castes, struck roots in the Tamil country along with the British colonial rulers hand-in-hand with them and exploited society. This essay rather forcefully points out how the brahmins with their 'prohit' (my preferred term for 'purohit' or priest) power and the vellala vaishyas with their political-economic power lorded over the shudras and the panchamar castes. (Here I would like to point out the distinction the French philosopher Roger Garaudy made between Prohit religion and Prophetic religion which facilitates oppression.)

Essay 5 on 'Dravidian Literature' (1995) is an introduction to the method adapted by the Dravidian writers in the struggle to invert the religious, caste, class and gender symbols of the hegemonic powers. The Dravidian parties which got degraded after coming to power were forces for social revolution before the 1960s. They ridiculed the hegemonic cultural symbols through their rebellious writings. The important aspect to remember here is that this parody and inversion comes in the continuum of Tamil literary tradition. The concept of Dialogism, proffered by the Russian linguist Mikhail Bakhtin, had not impacted the writing of Dravidian thinkers in any way. Though they drew inspiration from traditional Tamil folk literature, their own satire and ridicule generated laughter and celebration in their writings.

Essay 6 'Postmodernism and Dalit Ideology' (1997) was presented and debated in Manonmaniyam Sundaranar University at Tirunelveli. Marxism from the West was used as an ideological weapon for class analysis, class struggle and for destroying class itself in Tamil Nadu and in Sri Lanka. Similarly I have tried to use certain concepts from the Western, postmodern thoughts of Mikhail Bakhtin, Eva Tavour Bannet, Jean Baudrillard, Michel Foucault and Jacques Derrida for the annihilation of caste by understanding casteism and its class interaction that prevails in India and in Tamil Nadu. Though this is a novel attempt, it must be borne in mind that I have not disregarded Ambedkarism, historical materialism and dialectics.

Essay 7 'From the Subaltern Perspective: Re-Examination and Social Transformation' was first presented as a lecture at a seminar conducted by the Christian Studies Centre of the University of Madras and was later published in the journal *Uzhaipor Aayutham* (Weapon of Workers). It is about hill tribes, women, dalits who have been pushed to the margin. I have taken into consideration the various definitions of the term 'marginalized' from Antonio Gramsci to Ranajit Guha. I have engaged the criticisms of many non-dalits who are allergic to the emergence of the dalits. Women who occupy a central position in human reproduction and dalits and hill tribes, in material production, because of their birth and gender are all exploited as cheap labour. This essay tries to portray the manner in which they were shoved to the periphery by vicious means.

Essay 8 'Religion (Hinduism) from Dalit Perspective' was read at the seminar organized by the Guru Nanak chair in Madurai Kamaraj University. Through history, a vast number of working-class people have been suppressed on the basis of birth and untouchability and have been stigmatized as defiled people. Many take this lightly as a universal phenomenon. That way all the groups working on Human Rights issue need to be pitied. The collective power of the government ensures that their efforts remain ineffective. Any attempt at examining the origin of the caste system that prevails in South Asian societies is countered by vested interests. This is not the context to go into that aspect. The aim of this essay is to point out how the Prohit Hindu religion supports and justifies this graded caste structure and to see how the ideas of Iyothee Thass Pandithar (1845–1914), Babasaheb Ambedkar (1891–1956) and E. V. Ramasami Periyar (1879–1973) can help to understand the problem. Among the three, Iyothee

Thass and Ambedkar while speaking for dalit liberation criticized Hinduism. On the other hand, Periyar spoke from the plane of atheism and rationalism, for the liberation of the shudras, one of the four varnas (divided as forward, backward, and very backward castes).

Iyothee Thass and Ambedkar tried to expose the casteist-racist dimension of Hinduism. As an alternative to Hinduism they tried to build up a new Buddhism (Navayana), free of caste differences. Yet in the sincere efforts of all these three thinkers there was an inherent contradiction and it expressed itself even in their lifetimes. In Buddhism, which was offered as an alternative to caste-riddled Hinduism, casteism began to sprout among the Sri Lankans and the Indians. In spite of Periyar's rationalist, atheist logic, in the people who occupied the social position next to the brahmins, the caste issue came up. Moreover, since Periyar, unlike the two dalit leaders, did not have the annihilation of the caste system as his goal, caste flourished among the vellalas and the backward castes (shudras), to whom he belonged.

Whoever tries, unless they set out to plan a revolutionary strategem to eliminate the caste system, will find it difficult to eradicate caste divisions from the followers in South Asia of Hinduism, Islam, Jainism, Buddhism and Christianity. To put it briefly, if we ignore the prophetic religions and extol Humanism and believe in the Prohit religion which supports caste divisions, humanity can be deemed to be destroyed. All the above essays have this ideal as the goal. Maybe it will be achieved some time or it may remain a dream. Anything can happen in this universe. What can mere human beings do?

This book comes in the wake of the booklet 'Vedagama College and Dalits' (Oct. 1992). After reading this publication many readers wrote to me raising a number of issues. I hope I have answered their questions in this book to a certain extent. When I asked for an introduction to this English version of my book, V. Geetha agreed with alacrity and wrote a very appropriate piece, contextualizing my essays. She has been following my writings closely for which I am grateful to her. It is my good luck that Theodore Baskaran, a writer I respect very much, was available to translate my essays to form this collection. While working with him I realized that he was deeply involved with my writings and ideas contained in them.

Taking on all the daily domestic chores herself, my wife, Dr. K. Parimalam, made it possible for me to get fully involved in reading and writing. My love and gratitude to her for her unstinting support.

Raj Gauthaman
Puducherry
April 2020

Note

1 *Dalit Panpadu* (Dalit Culture, Puducherry: Gauri Pathipagam, 1993).

Translator's Note

THOUGH I HAVE been familiar with the writings of Raj Gauthaman for more than two decades, when I sat down to translate his works I found it difficult. The articles, addressed primarily to the Tamil-reading public and some of them on subjects new to them, had to be translated for an international readership. One point I had to bear in mind was that some concepts, unfamiliar to Tamil readers, which the author explains with great care and detail, are often already known to the readers in English: for instance, Foucault's ideas on hegemonic forces. These essays in this anthology were written at different points of time, spreading from 1992 to 2002. They are organized here in a chronological order so that the movements and contexts that the author was writing about will be clear. Some of the articles were presented in seminars and some appeared in literary magazines which means their tone and structure differ.

Raj Gauthaman, of course, thinks in Tamil and his writings are deeply rooted in the history and the culture of the land. So are the earthy metaphors, similes and idioms he so effectively employs. These had to be demystified while disseminating them in English. Add to this his writing style, which consists of long sentences with many clauses and sub-clauses and the whole process gets very complex. One had to break the syntax and release, as it were, the meanings contained in it and give them in English. I tried to get into his mind to make sense of some of the sentences.

His tone, expressions of anger, utter contempt for some long held beliefs and sarcasm that manifests in his writings, posed a challenge. I had to look at not only the meaning but also his style which has a bearing on the meaning. His style reflects his disrespect for polite, formal language. His use of pun and double entendres being so language-specific and culture-bound could hardly be translated. When he writes about dalit literature I find each word loaded and deeply embedded in dalit consciousness and it was my work to get at the kernel of this. His deep scholarship in classical Tamil literature and the terms he engages with while writing about it makes his writings on such subjects dense. His piece on re-reading of *Periyapuranam* (Essay 3) is one such. He is able to see beyond the mythological stories while deconstructing them.

I have always admired his writing and his commitment to equality in human life and to end the caste system. I consider it a privilege to get an opportunity to interpret Raj Gauthaman's writing and to make it accessible to a wider world of readers and scholars and also to the vast number of Tamils who cannot read Tamil. While working on this book I realized the truth of what Joseph F. Graham, Derrida's translator, wrote: 'Translation is an art of compromise; if only because the problems of translation have no one solution and none that is fully satisfactory. The best translation is merely better than the worst to some extent, more or less.'

I want to acknowledge my gratitude to Dr. Judith Heyer, economist, the University of Oxford, for having read all the chapters closely, pointing out errors and suggestions. The title *Dark Interiors* is taken from the caption of a line drawing done in 1992 by Achuthan Kudallur. I am thankful to him for the permission. One of India's foremost abstract painters, who was the Commissioner for the Tenth Indian International Triennial, New Delhi, and whose work is sold by Sotherby's and Christies's, he has graciously agreed to the use of his image for the book cover. The author, publishers and I are very appreciative of this. I am grateful to R. Prakash of Roja Muthiah Research Library, Chennai, for helping with the index.

S. Theodore Baskaran
Bengaluru
October 2019

Introduction

V. Geetha

RAJ GAUTHAMAN HAS been writing for well over thirty years. Brilliant and provocative, he has pushed the boundaries of Tamil literary criticism by imaginative readings of texts and contexts. The essays translated for this volume represent an important part of his work: writing that has engaged with dalit liberation politics and culture. The relationship of dalits to Tamil history and culture, and to the past and present of the Dravidian movement, the progress of non-brahmin politics in the state and what that has meant for dalits, the many strands that constitute radical dalit culture—these are some of the themes foregrounded in these essays.

Gauthaman has provided detailed descriptions of how each of these essays came to be written, including the year of its publication. This is important information because each bears the impress of its occasion and time and helps the reader understand the social and cultural circumstances which informed the publication and reception of these texts. This was the decade of the 1990s, which witnessed accelerated dalit assertion in Tamil Nadu, both in the political and cultural spheres. Writing, publishing, creating new standards of judging culture, organizing cultural festivals—dalit groups and individuals associated with Ambedkarite spaces, the far Left and with radical Church organizations were all involved in this process. It was a heady and exciting time and in retrospect it is clear that dalit intellectual activity of the 1990s redefined the terms of debate in the area of culture, particularly in the manner we receive and process literary texts.

These years also saw intellectuals, writers and fellow-travellers, associated with both parliamentary and radical Left parties reckoning with developments in the former Soviet Union and in Central Europe. Eventually, some of them came to rethink the class question. The journal *Nirapirigai* emerged as a forum to discuss and argue on these matters; class came to be considered in tandem with the caste question, on the one hand and in the context of other democratic struggles, to do with the environment, the women's question and civil rights campaigns, on the other. *Nirapirigai* also initiated a serious revisiting of Periyar's legacy and undertook a re-reading of Periyar—given that the late 1980s and the early 1990s saw renewed attacks against dalits in Tamil Nadu and protests against the Mandal Commission report elsewhere in India, such a re-reading appeared in order. All this granted a fillip to dalit assertion and, in turn, was affected by it.

Civil rights groups and women's organizations were also active throughout this period in an unprecedented sort of way and brought together men and women from different class and caste backgrounds, and with differing political beliefs. This made for provisional but exciting partnerships and sustained campaigns against state violence directed at dalits and women—witness, for instance, the public ire over the devastation of the tribal hamlet of Vachathi (1992); as also the widespread condemnation of the massacre of dalits in what has since come to be known as the Tamarabarani massacre (1999).

It would not be an exaggeration to note in this context that dalit political and cultural assertion deepened democratic and rights politics in the state and renewed our interest in the question of caste and opposition to the caste order. By the same token, some of the verities of the Tamil political world came to be questioned and created for the first time in decades a critical context to challenge the stifling consensus forged by the Dravidian political parties with respect to social justice, federalism and linguistic nationalism.

Gauthaman's work bears the impress of all these developments. His bold and programmatic essays on dalit culture and literature brought together issues at stake in debates set in motion by dalit writers and intellectuals as well as their interlocutors. His historical writing, to do with the Tamil non-brahmin vellala elites, took a caste lens to the Non-Brahmin movement and attempted to account for its limitations by looking to the medieval past—a turn to history that was initiated by *Nirapirigai*. His forays into epistemology, evident in his essay on postmodernism and on subalternity were of a part with other such attempts in the Tamil world of letters: structuralism and poststructuralism, as well as postmodernism were all important buzz words in the 1990s but there were also serious attempts to endow them with political charge. The *Nirapirigai* group worked hard to do the latter, and Gauthaman, who worked with the group, developed some of the ideas that were current at that time to his own purpose.

What is undoubtedly Gauthaman's own, and which informs all the essays in this volume, has to do with his understanding of gender—he is insistent that the caste order degrades dalits and women, and argues this with particular prescience in his essay on the *Periyapuranam*. While gender and feminism were themes that attracted attention in the 1990s, very few writers or critics engaged with them systematically and it is to Gauthaman's credit that he did so. Gauthaman's work, as presented in this volume belongs, as I have noted above, to the decade of the 1990s. His subsequent work, begun in the late 1990s and which continues to this day is equally exciting: it is less programmatic, and hinges on his close historical and critical reading of key Tamil literary and other texts. Replete with nuance and detail, the arguments he offers are yet concerned with broad issues to do with history and culture. There is a continuity too with past concerns, only these latter are refined and modified in significant ways.

In what follows, I suggest how the essays in this volume relate to his subsequent work.

The first three essays in the collection (1.'The Dalits of Tamil Nadu and Dalit Literature'; 2. 'Dalit Culture'; 3. '*Periyapuranam*: Hierarchy and Inversion') announce a common intent: they are concerned with defining the contours of an emergent dalit cultural sensibility and one that is determined to work against the grain of received wisdom about literature and history. Of the remaining essays, two have to do with method: the one on postmodernism and its relevance (6. 'Postmodernism and Dalit Ideology') and the other on the uses of subalternity (7. 'From the Subaltern Perspective: Re-examination and Social Transformation'). The essay on the vellalas (4. 'Brahmins, Vellalas and the Tamil Country') and on Dravidian literature (5. 'Dravidian Literature') deal with the phenomenon of Non-Brahminism, as a historical condition and in terms of how it responded to brahmin hegemony, politically and culturally. The eighth essay, as its title suggests has to deal with dalit religiousity ('Religion [Hinduism] from Dalit Perspective'). Taken together, these essays, including the last one on IyotheeThass, form a complex whole, with each speaking to the other, even as they address, in greater or lesser measure the following questions: What is worthwhile tradition when dalits come to claim the past? What histories may they draw upon and for what purposes? If all culture is informed by caste, what is and ought to be dalit culture?

The first essay, 'The Dalits of Tamil Nadu and Dalit Literature', rehearses themes that Gauthaman would recall and rework in the years to come. It reads as a veritable cultural manifesto, and its key arguments are elaborated in 'Dalit Culture', which offers a transgressive and defiant re-reading of Tamil cultural and literary history. Gauthaman is at his ironic and derisive best in this essay, as he sets out to measure and assess Tamil culture against the grain, as it were.

Given the Dravidian movement's mining of Tamil literary history to make a case for Tamil identity and culture being different and exceptional, literary texts bear a unique burden. They are often called upon to do service to the Tamil present, as well as proclaim the exceptional nature of the Tamil past, and its essential difference from all things Sanskrit, Aryan and brahminical. This is demanded especially of 'Sangam literature', that corpus of texts which have been collected into the *The Eight Anthologies* (எட்டுத்தொகை), the *Ten Idylls* (பத்துப்பாட்டு), and *The Minor Eighteen Anthology Series* (பதினென்கீழ்கணக்கு). Importantly, this investment in a Tamil past was seldom only celebratory. In the writings of anti-caste thinkers, particularly E. V. Ramasami Periyar and his circle, the Tamil past, indeed, all of culture was subjected to devastating and merciless criticism and parody.

Gauthaman's 'Dalit Culture' is marked by the second of these impulses. He submits culture as it has evolved in caste society to dismissive critique: Hinduism, brahminical ritual, thought and custom, Bakthi devotionalism, other faiths, such as Islam and Christianity which yet observe caste differences, secular political movements, such as the Non-Brahmin movement which claimed to be opposed to brahmin authority, but whose constituents continued to discriminate and oppress dalits, are all roundly criticized. Gauthaman points out that there are two moral orders at play in all of the above: one that enables dominant castes to set rules and moral norms that work in their favour; and another that sets up a coercive code of conduct for the dalits, who are expected to accept and abide by it. This makes it untenable for dalits to abide by what passes for culture or tradition.

Significantly, this grand rejection is not all: the second part of Chapter 2 'Dalit Culture' sounds the tocsin of dalit liberation. It insists that dalits look to their everyday practices of social affection, generosity and openness to forge a new self. It also makes a case for what Gauthaman calls 'inversion', standing caste proscriptions on their head. Drawing on

Periyar's dictum that sins and crimes under the order of caste are to be inverted, and that each of us has to turn criminal and sinner to upturn its pieties, Gauthaman suggests that to embrace the forbidden is an act of protest and an affirmation of what is derided.

Yet not all acts of inversion have the same valence. Gauthaman points to how inversion as strategy came up against its own limits in the literature that emerged in the wake of the Dravidian movement. In 'Dravidian Literature', he grants the historical importance of texts that criticized brahminical and caste norms, but notes that the countering of these latter in the name of self-respect, a presumed non-brahmin unity or even socialism, was never quite adequate to the task of opposing varnadharma. In other words, the annihilation of caste was not as marked in these texts as it ought to have been.

Chapter 4 'Brahmins, Vellala and the Tamil Country' helps us understand the possibilities as well as limits of non-brahmin opposition to the caste order. In this essay Gauthaman argues that historically, elite non-brahmin castes, such as the vellalas, forged an alliance with brahmins and Brahminism and this made for cultural compromise. This latter, he suggests, continues to shape and limit non-brahmin political and cultural assertion. Non-Brahminism to be sure is an important and historically necessary aspect of modern Tamil history, but it has been constrained by a past that has kept it tied to conventional notions of culture and literature.

Gauthaman's rejection of the past and culture is at once expansive and particular: that is, his conceptual framework is ambitious, but his analysis is grounded in a deep and keen knowledge of texts, contexts and their reception, as is evident in his reading in Essay 3 of the *Periyapuranam*. Here he argues that Bakthi has been conventionally viewed as a counter to orthodox authority but the question is whether it was at all redemptive. For, the hagiographic tradition that memorialized the lives of Saiva saints in the Tamil country made sure that salvation and caste status were intimately linked and mapped one onto the other. Measuring textual verities against the everyday lives of caste, Gauthaman demonstrates how caste is at once location, a shaper of subjectivity and resident in quotidian life, to do with food, dirt and touch. This everyday-ness, he argues, informs experiences of devotion, but is seldom granted literary salience. On the other hand, it compromises the transcendence of Bakthi, in fact, undermines it decisively.

It is this understanding of caste (Essay 6), as far as dalits are concerned. This is also what leads him to appropriate subaltern historical reasoning to his own purpose. Foucault, Baudrillard and Ranajit Guha (Essay 7) are all ushered into his conceptual world to clarify the importance of thinking beyond economic or social amelioration and to address issues to do with consciousness, habit, the irrational and history's contingent moments. While Gauthaman is keenly aware of the importance of rational and satiric critique, he is equally drawn to the possibilities of cultural difference, of what might be upheld in the face of conceptual and emotional violence and this is why he returns to the question of faith and faith-based ritualism as a resource for Dalits (8 'Religion [Hinduism] from the Dalit Perspective').

These essays represent one crucial axis of Gauthaman's thought: defiant rejection and criticism of all that exists, including, to an extent, existing dalit writing. On this basis, one is likely to conclude that his is an embittered view, leavened by a sense of utopian longing. But if one were to sketch in his other axis, profound critical engagement with what he derides the picture changes: his vision emerges as truly and generously dialectical.

Interestingly, even as he dismissed culture as such, as unworthy legacy for dalits, Gauthaman did not ever stop engaging with it. There were two kinds of engagement, one, that continues to this day, being an acute re-reading of the content of the Sangam corpus, and the other, a rigorous analysis of Tamil modernity, as manifest in the work of key authors and texts, from the last quarter of the nineteenth century.

An early volume, *Dalit Paarvayil Tamizh Illakiyam* (1993) took an unusual critical lens to the Sangam texts: the book unfolds as a series of conversations between a dalit intellectual, presumably Gauthaman, and a group of dalits. The 'intellectual' attempts to talk to the latter about Tamil literature, and the Sangam past, but he is interrupted by community elders who ask him what is specifically literary about texts that tell stories that they all know—stories of labouring people, their lives and loves. By skilfully assimilating the various references to work, love, sex and duty in the Sangam texts to the everyday lives of dalits in the present, Gauthaman brings it within the ken of a present that is not afraid of it, or awed by it. In effect, he demonstrates that dalits are the most worthy and embodied inheritors of the Sangam legacy.

Around the time that this book was published, that is, during the early 1990s, Tamil identity, and the idea of a Tamil nation were hotly debated in the Tamil public sphere (I have referred to this above). Dalit writers were in the forefront of this debate. The questions they raised were powerful and poignant: Does every Tamil have an equal claim on the putative Tamil nation? Does this nation engage with each of its constituents in equal measure, especially women and dalits? What sort of status could the latter expect to have in a future Tamil nation that is insufficiently committed to the rejection of patriarchy or caste? Gauthaman's claiming of the Sangam past as dalit history cut into the heart of this debate, and stood the question of Tamilness on its head. If Tamilness is essentially constituted by dalit labour and sensibility, all that is inimical to it is, by definition, not 'authentic'. In other words to claim to Tamilness and not oppose caste is simply not tenable or worthy.

In the years to come, Gauthaman would return to the Sangam texts, determined to claim them as worthwhile history in a rather oblique way. For him, this worth lay in the sensuous life-world the texts depicted, but which, as he demonstrated, had to be read off them. That is, they were not simply available to conventional or canonical interpretations. What Gauthaman chose to read in these texts was the following. He held the sensuousness of the worlds portrayed in the Sangam corpus to close scrutiny and argued that it existed as a crucial aspect of an inner erotic life, fundamental to female life experiences in the Sangam Age. He argued that the supersession of this inner life, with its emphasis on love and carnality, by a logic of (male-centred) production and control led to a taming and imprisoning of eros itself (an argument that he pursues, drawing on Nietzsche's *The Genealogy of Morals*, in several subsequent volumes). In turn, such taming brought about inequality, hierarchy and various forms of subordination.

These insights are gathered in two books: *Aram Adigaram*, an extensive study of Tamil morality, published first in 1998 and *Tamizh Samuthayathil Aramum Aattralum* (an expanded version of the former, published in December 2008). The first comprises analyses of ethical and epic literature, dating back to the third century CE, including Jaina and Buddhist texts. It raises a set of questions to do with the evolution of ethics in Tamil society: how did Tamil society come to be accord value to certain sorts of values and reject certain others? What were the acts mandated or suppressed or banished in the making of these values? If, for example, charity or gift-giving became a cherished aspect of kingly virtue, then what made this act of charity possible? Through what means did that hand that 'gave gifts position itself as morally superior to the hand that received them? What was the relationship of 'giving' and 'receiving' to royal authority? What sorts of edicts were proclaimed to regulate acts of gift-giving and receiving? In other words, through what means was the labouring hand tamed to become the receiving hand? How did the producing hand become the hand that came to control and rule?

Tamizh Samuthayathil Aramum Aattralum extends these arguments in another direction: it examines the latter day texts in the Sangam corpus to demonstrate how brahminical religious culture came to prevail within a recognizably Tamil universe. The clan-like existence of Sangam society within defined ecological niches, argues Gauthaman, eventually gave way to an unequal social and economic order held together by brahminical custom and royal authority. However the ideological consensus for the new order was wrought not by rejecting the Sangam corpus but by accommodating key aspects of that world within the terms of the new. The erotic charge of the past, for instance, was carried over into the new age, but was transformed to represent highly stylised forms of love and devotion. These latter reached their apogee in the figure of the viraha, or the lovelorn devotee, whose longing for the divine became the means through which brahminical gods and goddesses came to inhabit the Tamil universe.

Gauthaman makes clear that he is not scornful of historical memory. But he is clearly determined to 'remember' the past differently. He is neither nostalgic nor dismissive, neither romantic nor nihilistic: in his remembering, the past arrives marked by various lines of control, but he makes it clear that there is something of value in it, since it does represent a time and place when the caste order was not yet fully in place, and which bears the marks of another way of being and living.

Such a mode of engagement with what he construes to be problematic but which he nevertheless seeks to make his own is present in his approach to Tamil modernity as well. Here, we need to distinguish his readings of the great literary modernists, with his readings of the modern moment as such. In his reading of the great modern writers, A. Mathavaiya, Subramania Bharathi and Pudumaipithan, he does take a caste lens to their work and calls attention to how their upper-caste location limited their otherwise rich understanding in crucial ways. But he does not stop there. He goes on to draw a compelling and rich portrait of the inner imaginative world of these writers and claims the vigour and ecstatic nature of their imagination for dalit aesthetics. This is particularly the case with the long monograph he wrote on Pudumaipithan.

It might appear that these careful exercises in interpretation, of particular texts and authors contradict his earlier wholesale rejection of all culture as inimical to dalit freedom. It is important that these two ways of thinking about the past and culture are not seen as mutually contradictory. Clearly, they are held together in dialectical tension. For instance in the very first essay in this volume, 'The Dalits of Tamil Nadu and Dalit Literature' Gauthaman presents an analysis of literature (by non-dalits) that has dalits as protagonists or important characters and also of texts produced by dalit writers. His tone is angry, restless, and while his interpretations are not partisan, they are certainly not as nuanced as they could be—the reason is that his intent in this essay is to express, as he observes, 'a new alertness' that was visible in dalit expressions, in the Dr. Ambedkar Centenary year.

But in another brilliantly conceived essay, published a few years later (in 2003), on how dalits have been represented in modern Tamil fiction, we find him offering another sort of reading, no less critical, but less polemical. He groups representations of dalits by various writers under the following heads: dalits as the recipients of upper-caste benevolence; the dalit as a trope, to aid the progress of the plot, sharpen the moral of a tale; the dalit as a measure for others' morality; as villains, symbols of the 'low'; dalits in the context of conversion; dalit freedom in Hinduism; violence against dalits; as cheap labour. The point is there is a fine tension that marks his critical sensibility. His obvious relish of literary texts is held in check by a sharp analytical temper, but except when he wishes to be clearly programmatic, he is reluctant to privilege the one tone over the other. And even when he does, he is committed to claiming the aesthetic energy present even in texts that are ideologically compromised for a future dalit aesthetics.

Gauthaman's vision of the modern moment is as fascinating as his encounter with the great literary modernists. He conceives of it as an emergent moment, and one that is acutely present in texts which hearken back to a literary or religious past, while remaining alert and sensitive to the anxieties of the present, marked in this instance by greed, hunger, inequality, the promises of equality and a just society. Two remarkable texts may be cited in this context: one on the life and thought of the Saivite heretic, Ramalinga Adigalar, popularly known as Vallalar, and the other on the neo-Buddhist IyotheeThass Pandithar.

His understanding of Ramalinga Adigalar is finely ecumenical. He offers a reading of the man, his times and his work, each in terms of the other, and thereby narrates the making of a heretical persona, who lived on the cusp of an older devotional culture as well as an emergent democratic one, and whose last years were spent ministering to the needy and the sick, in ways that anticipated a brave new world, free from want and injustice. Once again we find Gauthaman displaying a mastery of texts that he ultimately rejects, in this case, the Saivite devotional corpus. He argues that Tamil Saivism represents a consensus wrought between (northern) Vedantic and (southern) Agamic faiths, and that Ramalinga Adigalar inherited this consensus but did not stay with it, instead he worked his way out of it, in response to the anxieties of the colonial era. In doing so, he inaugurated a new Tamil ethos, and one that would figure and re-figure in the thought and practice of all that came after, including Iyothee Thass and Periyar.

Gauthaman's study of Ramalinga Adigalar is of a part with his larger concerns: to do with religion and its influence on culture. In an unusual study on the *Tholkapiyam*, the oldest extant Tamil text on grammar and prosody, he argues that the Tamil cultural context fielded both brahminical and shramanic traditions with aplomb, and that the *Tholkapiyam* represents the Tamil response to these influences from the Sanskrit, Prakrit and Pali. He then goes on to note that Tamil Bakthi too has to be seen as doing the same: as representing a Tamil response to the pull of brahminical Hinduism (see above), wherein the sensuousness that is characteristic of the Sangam texts is called to do service to a hegemonic yet affective eros that helps bridge Tamil and non-Tamil religious worlds.

Another important text in this context is Gauthaman's study of Iyothee Thass (Essay 9). Gauthaman is drawn to how Thass deploys folk motifs and stories in his exposition of Tamil Buddhism, but he is equally fascinated with the Buddhist tradition's constitutive rationalism, evident in P. Lakshmi Narasu's work on the Buddha's life and message. Once again, we find him examining what the Tamil cultural world offers, as it turns its face to extraneous influences, but in this instance, he appears to want to uphold the claims of the latter as much as he affirms the former, that is, with respect to Buddhism as a creed that enables critique of the caste order, he is drawn to its rational and ethical aspects, even as he acknowledges the importance of grounding these latter in Tamil literary myth and legend.

Gauthaman's writing may be read as a fine instance of 'double-voiced discourse', to adapt a phrase from Mikhail Bakhtin. What one set of texts proclaims has to be heard over and against what another set claims, and within texts too, the dialogic imagination may be seen to be at play. This is why it appeared important to frame the essays translated for this volume in terms of other essays, addressing similar themes, but from different contexts and towards other purposes.

Chennai
July 2020

Books by Raj Gauthaman

Dalit Panpadu (Dalit Culture), Puducherry: Gowri Pathippagam, 1993.

Dalit Paarvayil Tamizh Panpaadu (Tamil Culture – A Dalit Perspective), Puducherry: Gowri Pathippagam, 1994.

Aa. Madavaiah, 1872–1925, Bengaluru: Kavya, 1995.

Pudumaipithan Ennum Brahmarakshas (A Brahmarakshas called Pudumai-pithan), Chennai: Tamizhini, 2000.

Arram Adigaram (Ethics/Power), Coimbatore: Vitiyal, 1997.

Kann Moodi Pazhakam Ellam Mannmoodi Poga: C. Ramalingam, 1823–1874 (That Blind Custom May Be Buried in Sand: C. Ramalingam, 1823–1874), Chennai: Tamizhini, 2001.

Dalitiya Vimarasana Katturaigal (Critical Essays on Dalitism), Nagercoil: Kalachuvadu, 2003.

Kaa. Iyothee Thass Aaivugal (Kaa. Iyothee Thass: An Enquiry), Nagercoil: Kalachuvadu, 2004.

Tamizh Samuthayathil Arramum Aattralum (Ethics and Capabilities in Tamil Society), Coimbatore: Vitiyal, 2008.

Pattum Thogaiyum: Tholkappiyamum Thamizh Samooga Uruvakkamum (Idyll and Anthology: Tholkappiyam and the Making of Tamil Society), Chennai: Tamizhini, 2008.

1

The Dalits of
Tamil Nadu and Dalit Literature

I WOULD LIKE to begin this essay with what the French Catholic priest J. A. Abbé Dubois (1765–1848) said about the pariahs of South India.[1] He wrote:

Pariahs drink toddy.
Filthy folks. Have no sense of honour.
They constantly fight. And beat
Their wives. They eat the carcass of ox.
The huts they live in are sources of diseases.
If their population increases, barbarism will
Rule the land.

After the above description, the term 'paraiyan' that was in use in India as an abusive term gained currency all over the world. There are large numbers of people of these castes in Tamil Nadu. In this essay the term 'pariah' is used to denote all of these castes.[2] If we are to use any other term to refer to these people, we have to use the word 'dalit' which is a term from another language.

From the time when literature appeared in India, in all the works written by upper-caste people there are only denigrating references to dalits. They were called 'low-born' and different from the 'peaceful' (*aaniyal*) twice-born brahmins (*purananooru*).[3] The epics associated these people

1

with theft, meat-eating, dishonesty and whoring. Saint-poet
Appar, author of *Thevaram*, talked about dalits and lepers
in one breath. In the inscriptions of the Chola, Pandya and
Nayaka periods, they are referred to as 'low born'. They had
separate crematoria (*parai sudukadu*) and separate wells
(*parai kulakuzhi*) for their use. Their habitats were near
crematoria and near lakes and paddy fields. Like the cats
raised in the harem, and the elephant tied outside the town,
while the oligarchs lived in proper settlements, the dalits
who worked for them lived outside (*cheri*).[4]

Caste Politics in South India during the European Period

When the Europeans landed on the Indian coast, with the
Bible in one hand and a sword in the other, and eventually
started ruling the land, caste politics was at work in the Tamil
country. After they gained a foothold, it was the brahmins
who first tasted the new power in the Tamil country. In
the early years they would not even go near the white man
who fed on beef prepared by pariah cooks. Though the
brahmins initially referred to the white man's language as
'the unclean tongue' and 'pariah tongue' they soon changed
their attitude. Some of them who learnt English projected
themselves as progressive by drinking coffee and eating meat
at eateries where the cooks were pariahs. During the sixty
years from the time of the Sepoy Mutiny (1857) to the time
when Gandhi assumed the political leadership of the national
movement, that is, till the appearance of the Justice Party of
the Tamil-Telugu vellalas, brahmins were in the majority in
government jobs and in the legal profession. The next lot of
hegemonic castes were Tamil-Telugu vellalas. After imbibing
egalitarian ideas through European literature, brahmins
began demanding equal treatment with the English. They
attempted to reform Hinduism to make it like Christianity.
Just as brahmins took the Englishman as a model for
equality, the educated Tamil vellalas took brahmins, who

were above them, as the models and declared that there was no caste inequality. To break the authority brahmins had gained during British rule, the vellalas used two devices. These devices came in handy to view themselves as the equal of brahmins and to gather those Tamil caste people below them under the rubric 'non-brahmin'.

The First Device

Vellalas who grew acquainted with the ideas of equality through Western education, rejected the hegemony of brahmins. During colonial rule, vellalas tried various approaches to elevate themselves to the status of brahmins. For this purpose they operated in different planes such as religion, religious education, Western education, culture, creating of local legends, popular literature, vegetarianism, rituals, trusteeship in temples, and so on. On the one hand they promoted themselves to be equal to brahmins and on the other tried to lead the Dravidian Adi Dravida castes. Through Hinduism, Puranas, folk literature, language and race, they created myths to support their stand. Simultaneously they tried to earn for themselves a religious role by creating folklores and mythologies. Such fabrications were used to bring together the Dravidian castes that were beneath them in the hierarchy and promote Dravidian ideology. They made sure that the dalits had a separate identity called Adi Dravida.

The Second Device

In the bourgeois democracy introduced by the British, representative politics facilitates the capture of power through the support of the majority. To oppose the brahmins who were just 2 percent of the Tamil people, the vellalas tried to bring the rest of the 98 percent under the category of Dravidians. The Tamil language and Saivism also came in handy for the caste politics of the vellalas.[5]

The vellalas are as responsible as the brahmins for making dalits untouchables. Yet, the vellalas accused the brahmins and their Sanskritic culture of being accountable for the crime of untouchability. Individuals like Nilāmbigai Ammaiyar pointed to the brahmins as the cause of untouchability while she herself had her feet deep in brahminical Sanskritic culture.[6]

The Justice Party was formed with the purpose of gathering castes from the shudra vellalas (Dravidians) and the rest of the vast majority of oppressed castes of the dalits. The leadership of the Justice Party was in the hands of Telugu kulaks and Tamil vellalas. In this party were also a small number of educated pariahs who migrated to the cities and formed the Pariah Mahajana Sabha in 1890. Later, the same organization found a new name, Adi Dravidar Mahajana Sabai, as part of the new terminology of Dravidian politics. Quite a few dalits who were in the forefront of this organization (M. C. Raja, Rettamalai Srinivasan, V. I. Munuswamy Pillai, Dharmalingam Pillai and N. Sivaraj) were also members of the Justice Party.[7]

When the Indian National Congress gradually spread as a mass movement in the Madras Presidency, the Justice Party rejected the demand of Swarajya (self-rule) which it put forward. The dalits who were in the Justice Party also rejected this idea. The vellalas feared that if self-rule was granted, the hegemony of the brahmins who already held positions of authority in the government and other related organizations would persist. Similarly the atrocities relating to untouchability would also continue. The dalits informed the Indian National Congress that only after getting higher education would they consider joining the struggle for freedom.[8]

Though in the political context of that period the stand of the dalits sounded reasonable, they were in fact unwittingly supporting the political ascent of Telugu-Malayali-Tamil vellalas who treated the untouchables like animals, just as the brahmins did. But the educated dalits were only a small group who lived in cities: earth diggers, salt workers and

Pallars who tried to elevate themselves by re-christenings like Devendra Kula Vellalars, the Valluvars who did the rituals for all the above castes, and the beef-eating pariahs, were not able to gather under one-party flag and could not have dreamt of all the dalits getting together in those days.

While this was the situation in the cities, in the villages, a large number of dalits converted to Christianity and Islam to escape from starvation and from the torment of upper-caste Hindus. But even in the new fold, they were treated like slaves by the converted vellala-shudra caste people and some Muslims. Whether through the caste politics of vellalas, or by religious conversion, liberation for dalits remained a mirage. This is what history points out. Dalits should realize that they themselves will have to change their destiny. If they think that some other saviour will come and change it, they will never approach liberation.

Impact of Caste, Family and Religion

Before they seek liberation, dalits should carefully study the factors that made them untouchables and menials. They should examine how the upper castes gained authority to subdue them. In this caste-based society, and in the family, Hinduism has set up a hierarchy with inequality as the foundation. The hierarchical structure of Hinduism and the doctrine of karma have been formulated to make it appear as if each human being has chosen and internalized an economic structure with exploitation as its basis. The ideology of the family was formulated to make economic exploitation appear to be just. The Sastras of Hinduism created the rules regarding this. The rules implemented by Hinduism about the food eaten by the family, the manner of cooking it and who can eat with whom, made the majority of the people untouchables.[9] Vegetarian food, cow's milk and ghee became the identity of the upper castes while non-vegetarian food, particularly beef and pork, became the identity of low castes.

In upper-caste Hindu families, even at the age of one or two, children are taught what is polluting on the basis of food and who untouchables are. It is pointed out that the things connected with the cow are considered clean and those associated with the dog and the pig unclean.

> One can hold the tail of a cow
> And cross a river: can one hang on a dog's tail
> And cross a river?

says the Tamil ethical work *Aranericharam.*

> Can a dog that can eat and digest a bone
> Consume ghee and digest it?

asks another ethical work *Needhi Venba.* Underlying these questions is the dichotomy of clean and unclean associated with the cow and the dog. In ancient literature like *Purananooru,* brahmins, and virtuous women committed to one man are mentioned along with the cow. To the vellala, brahmin devotees who plead with God saying

> 'Worthless Pulaiah that I am'

and

> 'I am a dog, I am a pulaiah.'

in order to humble themselves, the lowliest creatures are the dogs, the dalit and the pulaiah. The urine of cows was considered sacred. When a Hindu was ostracized from his caste, it was the practice to drink a mixture of cow's dung, urine, milk, curds and ghee as atonement.[10]

The ritualistic rules framed on the basis of food, were used to maintain the pre-eminence of caste. If someone believed in caste superiority, he had to adhere to the ritualistic rules of his caste. The vellala leader Nallur Arumuga Navalar of

Jaffna said that eating with lower-caste people, meat-eating and drinking, violate these ritualistic rules.

In a Hindu family there were pollutants other than those identified on the basis of nourishment. People who handled beef, hides and toddy were declared untouchable. Similarly those whose livelihood was to clean were also declared untouchables; landless people, without even the implements to work in the field who eked out a living by cleaning jobs.[11] Those who cleaned garbage thrown into the streets by upper-caste Hindus and human excreta by the side of the road were considered contaminated. Those who ate the carcasses of cattle and those who disposed of the dead of the caste Hindus were all labelled untouchables. Similarly a woman member of a family who worked for the household was considered lower than others. Her nudity, her genitals and the discharges from them were considered impure. In the society and in the family, upper castes and males gained authority by subjugating women on the basis of sex. But the terms denoting a man's penis, and the acts of sex he indulged in, were used as symbols of supremacy.

A statement in the Hindu Sastras:

> For one who eats beef
> And for the brahmin who cohabits with a pariah woman
> There is no atonement.

This underlines the Hindu perspective which equates a dalit and a woman. In the olden days the punishment meted out by caste panchayats to a woman who violated the code of conduct and to a dalit who had broken caste rules was similar.

Even intercourse with a woman was described as an act of pollution by the Hindu Sastras. It was said that sexual contact with a woman, caused a man to lose his power of soul. Many rules, restrictions and guidelines were prescribed concerning sexual intercourse. Though it was laid down that a man should not sleep with any woman other than his wife, Hindu society created a class of women for extramarital relations.

According to the Sastras, a man may not have relations with his wife during menstruation, or on a new moon day or a full moon day. If he did, his body and soul would degenerate. Fulfilling a woman's sexual needs was looked upon as a boon from a man given at his will. The ethical rules laid down that if a man slept with a domestic help his honour and social status would be ruined and if he had sex with a prostitute, he would eventually lose his wealth.[12] Therefore it was wise for a wife to be a servant to her husband and a whore in bed. If he had sex with a widow, his lifespan would be reduced. When the sexuality of a woman is suppressed, the sexuality of the man also gets subdued. The sexual contact a man has with a whore, a servant, a widow or a woman from a low caste is an expression of suppressed sexuality. On the other hand, it was believed that the suppressed sexuality of a man through celibacy, yoga or penance added to his energy. Shunning women was held as progress on the spiritual path of a man. Eschewing sex was glorified as a sign of strength. Those who abjured sex and replaced it with worship of deities were hailed as having attained sacred authority.

The male anxiety of losing semen was equated with the fear of losing spiritual power. The Sanskritization of a caste can be gauged from the extent of its vegetarian food practices and the extent to which its men eschew the sex act (Lannoy).[13] The rules of sexual contact and the codes of pollution were used to bestow authority on upper-caste men. The same rules enabled hegemonic control to be wielded directly over women and indirectly over dalits. This can be clarified through an example. In the sixteenth and seventeenth centuries, in the Chettinad area, a poet called Mangaikavirayar, who was part of the tradition of distinguished poets, wrote ten songs ridiculing one Chattanathan, a wealthy man, who had mocked him. In those songs, titled *Chattanathan Pillai Thamizh,* the poet used what people from the caste-based society of that time considered contemptible acts to disparage him. He mocked Chattanathan as the 'son of a prostitute', and his wife and daughters as 'adulteresses', saying that his wife had sex with other men and that his food was prepared from the urine and menstrual discharge of servants.

Such outbursts of scorn come out as an expression of sexual subjugation. When the poet derided Chattanathan he described him as associated with potters, pulaiyars, and cobblers, the dogs of the slums, the drums of the pariahs and the penis of a barbarian. These are also expressions of casteist oppression. Therefore, in the caste structure of Hinduism, sexual and casteist suppressions are linked. Working women and dalits, in the family and in society (sometimes in both) are subjugated. The hard work of the dalits and the services rendered by women are taken advantage of by upper-caste men and established as sexual power. The concept of private property and the structure of the family have grown into a patriarchal set up. Women became a part of the property of men. It was sexual subjugation which made this possible. To ensure that men's possessions went only to their heirs, the sexual conduct of women was stressed and regularized. In the non-egalitarian caste structure, sexual subjugation among the upper castes took the form of the suppression of women and dalits through the codes of pollution. The similarity between the authority the upper castes gained by exploiting dalits and the power gained by men through the sexual exploitation of women in the domestic situation should be clearly understood. In the family all kinds of authorities are internalized psychologically by the individuals only on a sexual basis. As they demolish caste and economic supremacy dalits should end sexual authority at the domestic level.

The arguments given so far indicate the way to dalit liberation. Organized religion institutionalizes the family with its patriarchy and related caste structure that nurses upper-caste authority. Only when that is demolished, the liberation for dalits, along with others in the society, can be accomplished. Mere political and economic changes cannot bring about total liberation in a casteist and sexually controlled society.

Dalit Literature in Tamil

Let us look at dalit literature in Tamil in the context of what has been discussed in the above three sections.[14] While doing so, we have to bear in mind the fact that there is no such category as dalit literature in Tamil. The common understanding of dalit literature is that it is protest literature. Today there are quite a few protest literatures in Tamil. We will see in this section that all protest literature cannot be categorized as dalit literature. The majority of protest literatures while opposing the suppression of one section of society, in their turn tried to subdue another. This is because they look upon the problem of one section of society as that of the whole society. It is a holistic view.

The protest culture that raised its voice against alien imperialism supported the Gandhian platform and struggle on behalf of the workers. But later, after Independence, when Indian capitalists gained power, it began preaching that we should not agitate, but should work for the nation and move towards achieving our ideals. It held that the organization of society was fine; only a few were corrupt and selfish and that if we could change those, things would be all right. These ideas were mouthed by the polygamous heroes of Tamil writer Akilan, the white kurta-clad, curly haired, soft-footed protagonists of Na. Parthasarathy and the dhoti-clad Dravidian heroes of Mu.Varadarasan.

In the 1950s and 1960s, Dravidian protest literature featured the 'saintly poor' as the hero. The farmhands working for the kulaks, the cartmen, the marginalized in the cities, the rickshawpuller, and garbage collectors, prostitutes, widows and orphans acquired this saintly poor image. In Dravidian literature intended against the white khadar-clad rulers, the non-Congress vellalas set up the saintly poor as the leader of the downtrodden against the brahmin-vellala Congress. But his caste identity was carefully hidden. He was identified as the marginalized Tamilian. But when this Tamilian in the garb of the saintly poor came to power, 44 dalits were burnt alive in Keezhvenmani village in 1968 when they demanded higher wages.

Jayakanthan, after making coolies the lead characters of his stories in the style of Pudumaipithan and Vindhan, wrote about the private lives of brahmin women. In the eyes of the Dravidian and Communist youngsters he was a rebel. But eventually Jayakanthan announced that the brahmin and the pariah were one and ended up singing the praise of Sankarachariar. The Hindu concept of the ascending order of the doctrine of karma can be seen in Jayakanthan.

In the literature of the Communist Party, the saintly poor created by Dravidian literature were clad in red shirts. Caste identity was concealed. In their red shirts, the poor people countered the capitalists and opposed the landlords. They resisted the police and opposed the establishment. Of all the protest literature of Tamil, it was the literature of the Communist Party which raised its voice against the whole establishment. However, focusing on class struggle, it did not pay attention to family and caste. The saintly poor among the economically backward (BC group) now and then transcended their political identity and revealed their caste. They burnt the huts of the saintly poor below them. They raped their women. They killed their men and cattle together.

All the Tamil protest literature described above, while contesting one form of oppression, concealed or nursed another form. So where is the place for dalit literature here? A literature which resists all kinds of oppressions with an aim to create a situation where there is no oppression at all can be called dalit literature. But it cannot be said that only those born dalits can create this literature. If a political stand is taken to demolish caste, religion, the family based on sexual domination, and the economics of exploitation, and if it functions to destroy these, then it can be called dalit literature. All those who are ideologically dalits and who subscribe to this politics can create dalit literature.

It is the practice of writers in Tamil who write about the origin and growth of any idea, to trace it to a formula in *Tholkapiyam*, a circa AD fifth century grammatical treatise. But the origin of dalit literature cannot to be traced in that manner. Only in the coming years can its origin and progress be traced. British rule sowed the seeds for major social changes. It is futile to look for dalit literature in the period prior to colonial rule when Tamil literature concerned itself mainly with deities and kings. If there is any reference to dalits in this period, they may only be dalits by birth but ideologically will stand on the side of brahmin-vellalas. Nandanar is a good example. Characters like Nandan and Kannappan, by abandoning the deities of dalits, worship the gods of Saiva vellalas and brahmins. By doing so they appear to consider themselves liberated from 'lowly birth'.

In folk literature, particularly in the sixteenth, seventeenth and eighteenth centuries, the sad plight of the dalits, marginalized by caste Hindus, expressed itself through ballads. Though some dalit leaders killed by the dominant caste people were deified and worshipped as folk deities, dalits could not start a resistance movement. Folk deities Madurai Veeran (of Chakkliars) and Annanmar Swami (of pariahs) served the hegemonic castes.

The various dimensions of folk literature, however, can be used to create dalit literature. Folk literature is shorn of the glitter and shine of epics. One finds direct and hard hitting assertions. It does not shy away from matters relating to sexual relations. In vellalla literary works like *Kutralakuravanji* or *Mukootarpallu*, which have many characteristics of folk literature, Pallar and Kurava caste men and women characters indulge in explicit sexual innuendos and highly erotic talk, the kind of language that upper-caste people cannot stand. We have discussed earlier how suppressing sexuality or sanctifying it as ecstasy both create authority. So dalit literature should learn from folk literature to write without either subduing or sanctifying sexuality. What the caste Hindus glorified as sacrosanct in religion, caste and family systems brought authority to themselves and slavery to women and dalits. It is suicidal for dalits to exalt such sanctities. They have to demolish them and take care not to create new ones.

In the nineteenth century, Gopalakrishna Bharathi wrote the old story of Nandan, a dalit farmhand who becomes a devotee of Siva, under the title *Nandanar Sarithira Keerthanaigal* (History of Nandan) in lyrics. These songs became very popular, like film songs. Later, Puthumaipithan also wrote about Nandan in his short stories. Rajaji wrote a short story about a Harijan who goes after a woman as if proving his caste prediction. But all these were attempts to make a brahmin out of a pariah. A dalit has to move towards the high position of the vellala and the brahmin. Caste Hindus pointed out that this was the only way to transcend his lowliness. Ideologically only if everyone becomes a pariah or a dalit can we do away with any kind of casteist, sexual subjugation. Till then all this talk about everyone being of one clan and all being children of God is a mere fraud. Or we are so ignorant that we do not realize that it is an outright hoax.

During British rule, along with the ideology of hegemonic Hindus, came a European concept as well. In European bourgeois ideology, the private individual became the centre of focus and was identified as an independent being who could move forward by his own efforts. Hinduism with its Sanathana dharma held that if one strictly adhered to the rules of one's caste, one could gradually escape the cycle of birth and ultimately unite with the divine. In other words, even pariahs if they follow the rules of their caste, could go to the next higher caste, and repeating this in each birth, finally be born brahmins with a better chance of reaching God. This idea of liberation, with the brahmin as the ideal, can be seen in early Tamil novels and even in many contemporary stories.

Rajam Krishnan wrote about 'lowly' people like the Badagars of the Nilgiris in her novel. In her novels, spun around middle-class urban women, one can hear the echoes of humanitarian ideas familiar to city dwellers. Hill people and dalits who appear in her novels are depicted in an alienated manner, as if they come from some remote African jungle. Writing about Indira Parthasarathy's novel *Kuruthipunal* (Flood of Blood) dealing with the massacre of 43 dalits writer and critic Ambai commented that if vellala penises functioned well there would be no dalit massacre. We get a 'psychological' insight that there would have been no need to burn them alive. This is a problem with writers who get familiar with half-baked Freudian ideas through the books they get in city libraries and try to comment on the caste struggle that goes on in rural areas with which they are totally unconcerned. Those who delight in the new insights they gain through their research cannot contribute to dalit literature in any way.

In this context the progression of Poomani as a writer is amazing. In the beginning he wrote about Chakkiliyars as individuals from a humanitarian angle. At the same time he also pointed out that there are good men like Kandhaiya Naidu in dominant castes. Chakkiliyar versus Naidu problems are presented as difficulties among individuals. Even in his first novel, *Piragu* (Afterwards) he sacrificed the dalit cause at the altar of credibility of characters, realism and altruistic ideology. And dalits disappeared altogether in his second novel *Vekkai* (Heat). Nameless small-time landlords appear without any caste identity, as people divided on an economic basis. They play and kill each other over land. They raise dogs. As brothers, fathers, uncles and aunts they wallow in familial bonds.

In Poomani's next novel *Naivethiyam* (Puja) even these people vanish and brahmins make their appearance. The journey that began with Chakkiliyars and ended with brahmins is reflective of the Hindu obsession with crossing the cycles of birth to reach the divinehood of upper caste.

All the three novels of Poomani: *Piragu*, *Vekkai* and *Naivethiyam* demonstrate this trajectory. (*Vekkai* was made into a successful film under the title *Asuran* in 2019.) Among Sri Lankan Tamil writers, Daniel's novel *Kanal* (Mirage) is about Hindu dalits who convert to Christianity to escape the hands of Kamakarar and continue to suffer. He goes on to write about dalits who without resorting to conversion, get together and fight the vellalas. In the 1980s, Mark Stephen, a Tamil writer, wrote about the plight of Christian dalits who were led in their struggle against Christian leadership by an enlightened pastor. While Daniel held that it is pointless to convert in order to escape caste oppression, Mark Stephen in his novel *Yathirai* (Pilgrimage) advocated fighting the leadership within the Catholic Christian establishment.

In fact, Catholicism in India is nothing but Hinduism in the garb of suit, hat and veil. The temple became the church, the chariot morphed into the chapparam; Mariaatha became 'Mary matha' and Sudalaimadan and Karupuswamy became St. Sebastian and St. Antony. In both religions there are places and days for the sacrifice of goats and roosters. While Daniel took the stand that it is futile to try and reform caste and religion in general, Mark Stephen focused on protest within the establishment. However, I feel that dalits should reject both because whatever the sect, they are under subjugation. Both of these writers were sincere in their aim of dalit liberation and wrote with concern. But both were caught up in an ideological web and were therefore unable to formulate a complete dalit ideology in literature/their writings.

In this context, we will have to take a closer look at what writers like these two have to offer. Their stories are similar to the formula stories written solely for commercial purposes. The purpose is to make them accessible even to the lowbrow reader. One group wants their ideas to spread among the readers through their stories. The other would like to earn fame and wealth quickly. Instead of approaching sex and violence from a radical political angle, the peddlars of writing will produce varied stories to suite people's tastes, garnishing their work with sex, murder and rape. They hide real life under a false façade. One need not go into the counter revolutionary culture that such writings would create.

Those who resort to such formula stories while writing about dalits should bear in mind that they will only pass on depraved ideas to their readers. Whatever our subject, the form we choose is critical. Every political ideology has an appropriate form to encapsulate it. The literary forms are not innocent as they appear. Literary forms like novels and short stories that are related to the liberation of bourgeois society can be used by dalit writers. In addition, dalit literature has to choose a form that facilitates the confrontation of caste configurations and the family set up that is based on sexual suppression along with the social and economic structure of bourgeois society. It has to choose a form that is suitable for this purpose.

Dalit literature should raise its voice against all kinds of violence perpetrated by history against dalits, and the authoritarian establishment that makes this possible. Dalits have the right and need to deny caste and religion because there is no caste below the dalit. And there is no religion to defend her/him. The main thrust of dalit literature should be to destroy caste, religion and the male-centred family structure. In this matter, black literature, feminist literature and folk literature can provide models for dalit literature. A dreadful development can be observed. Dalits who are subjugated, internalize as their own the ideology of the very people who subjugated them. The present situation is conducive to the goals of the dominant people. Dalits have to act to change this. No one else will. It is wrong to say that economic liberation and equality will bring in a change. The fruits of economic revolution will be consumed by caste, religion and family worms. These worms have great powers of persistence. If the working class is to realize its goal of wiping out class distinctions, it can be achieved only by a movement of dalits to annihilate caste, religion and family.

Dalit literature is not for the pleasure of reading. It should disturb the reader. It should embarrass him or her It should expose the hidden caste-religion ideology in those who declare that caste and religion no longer operate in contemporary life. It should sicken them. Crushed people do not care about grace and manners. The heart and eyes of the reader should redden. Only then might we say that dalit literature has arrived.

Notes

1 Abbé J. A. Dubois, *Hindu Manners, Customs and Ceremonies* (Oxford: Oxford University Press, 1899). He fled France to escape the terror of the French Revolution and lived in South India from 1792 to 1823 as a missionary, spending many years in Srirangapatinam near Mysore.

2 Though there are many castes that are subjected to the atrocious practice of untouchability, the term 'paraiya' used to collectively denote all of them. Rather than the term 'dalit', the word that is used as an expletive, 'paraiya', may be used for this purpose, though the term is used much more specifically to denote one of the three major dalit caste groups in Tamil Nadu even today.

3 Aaniyal – Aan + Iyal Aan – cow. Peaceful as a cow. Bovine. *Purananooru.* 9:1.

4 Noboru Karashima, *South Indian History and Society: Studies from Inscriptions AD 850–1801* (New Delhi: Oxford University Press, 1984).

5 The term 'vellala' is used here as a collective noun to cover the non-brahmin Hindu castes of Pillai, Mudaliyar, Odyar, Chettiyar and Naidu. Maraimalai Adigal referred to them as vellalas.

6 This metaphor is seen in *Neethi Neri Vilakkam.* Neelambikai, who subscribed to the ideas of her father, made this statement. However, during her wedding a brahmin officiated in the rituals.

7 The suffix 'Pillai' is not an indication of being a vellala. In those times, many dalits took this suffix. The Kallars of Tanjore district declared themselves as 'Pillai'.

8 The debate between M. C. Raja and Thiru.Vi. Kalyanasundaram.

9 M. Monier Williams, *Indian Wisdom or Examples of the Religious, Philosophical and Ethical Doctrines of the Hindus* (Cambridge: Cambridge University Press [1875], 2010).

10 See Dubois, *Hindu Manners, Customs and Ceremonies*: 42–43.

11 Richard Lannoy, *The Speaking Tree: A Study of Indian Culture and Society* (Oxford: Oxford University Press,1971).

12 In the film *Ape and Super Ape* (1972) by Dutch documentary filmmaker Bert Haanstra, a group of female gorillas, approach the male leader of the troupe and show their genitals to acknowledge his dominance. The sexual origin of authority is shown here.

13 Lannoy, *The Speaking Tree.*

14 The reader to bear in mind that this essay was written in 1994.

2

Dalit Culture

I

Brahminic Hindu Culture

How can any change happen when the mind of every Hindu
is so tightly wrapped up in caste? When their whole lives are
spent in disentangling which caste is above them and which
below, and in secretly nursing desires to somehow advance
in the hierarchy and become brahmins, no one can change
the Hindus of our country. Karl Marx nor even his grand-
father can do anything. The Hindu can never be a human
being. Caste is his main identity. No one can save a Hindu
from caste.

In every nation there have been inequalities and beliefs
on pollutions and taboos. But nowhere do you get an
instance as in our society where a vast majority of people are
labelled as polluted and unclean on the basis of their birth,
and then treated as unequals; as low rather than high. In
Hindu casteist society there is no concept of equality. One
can only see the Hindu as little man-big man, the high and
the low, the polluted and the pure, guru and disciple, and so
on. Never can you see any caste Hindu as a 'good' man.
Hindu culture is the culture of priesthood. They created the
Vedas, brahminic ideology, Sutras, Smrithis, Dharmasastras,
Puranas and the Ithihasas. Though mythology and Puranas
appeared in the West also, in Greece they were created by

19

artists, poets and philosophers. This is a key distinction. The brahmin priests made others cultivate, fight wars, trade, do all manual work while they themselves indulged in ceremonies like yagna and created an ideology suited to this arrangement. They said there are two kinds of deities: one in heaven and the other on earth. They claimed that they were the deities on earth. God resides in the Vedas and since the brahmin priests have become proficient in the Vedas, God resides in them. The material presented during yagnas was divided into two. They claimed that material *(pinda)* put in the flames was for the gods and the other material *nivedhanam and dhanam* was for them, the gods on earth (Pusurar). Only if brahmins are satisfied, will other human beings get happiness in the next birth. Chandogya Upanishad describes brahmin priests doing yagna and eking out a livelihood as follows:

> A row of white dogs, catching each other's tail, go, and after sitting down they chant: 'Om! We will drink. Varuna! Prajapathi! Savithri! Feed us. O God of food! Feed us! Om!'[1]

Even today when a devotee goes to a temple to worship, he has the brahmin priest in mind. He thinks that he/she will not get salvation without the priest. All those who live inside the caste system of Hindu society lead a life that depends on another person. Brahmin priesthood has organized the whole society so that it is oriented towards its comforts. Brahmin priests have fashioned a hierarchical structure in which each stratum jostles with the other for status and prestige. They have thus created a culture of constant bickering.

What is strange here is that they believe that in this Kaliyuga to attain liberation they have to undergo so many cleansing rituals, atonements, appeasements, and vows from dawn to dusk. But the other shudras (not dalits, who are panchamar and not Hindus) need not go through all these tough rituals; they can attain salvation if they do chores and errands. This is a clever explanation and encouragement for manual work.

Caste Hindus in Tamil Nadu

Two thousand years ago brahmins coming from the north brought to Tamil-speaking areas, vedic hegemonic culture that stigmatized human beings, won the kings of the area to their side and began harvesting the benefits. During the time of the Pallava kings, the Pandyas (BC 300–900 AD), the Cholas (AD 900–1200), the later Pandyas and the Nayaks, the landlords accepted brahminic Hindu culture and in the process ruined the land. Landlordism that prevailed in the area supported their hegemony. Though vellala caste groups took the lead in this power structure, their position was decided by the brahmins who cited the Sastras to claim that they, the upper castes, were born out of the mouth of Brahma and on that basis had acquired the power to decide the position of each group. Temples, rituals, priesthoods all bestowed leadership and power on brahmin priests on religious grounds. Temples emerged as symbols of hegemony, the sanctum of brahmin priests. It was made clear that if other castes wanted to worship, the help of a brahmin was indispensable. People from all castes believed that in the temples built by craftsmen and labourers of the lower strata of society, and from the wealth of the kings and grants from landlords, ultimately the brahmin priest had to light the lamp and perform the rituals to sanctify them. Even now this is what they believe. The brahmin has the right to stand near the deity. Next to him on the basis of ownership of materials and connections with the temple, landlords, traders, artisans and others take their place in a hierarchy.

Hindu society functioned on the belief that only through a brahmin can one set one's eyes on the idol, worship and attain salvation. Indian Catholic Christianity is no better. It has been laid down that only through the priest, through the mass he conducts, can people attain salvation. When you observe that these Christian priests are mostly from the dominant castes such as Pillai and Reddy it is clear that the brahminic principles of Hinduism operate in Christianity also.

Dominant Castes and Classes

By giving grants to brahmins, to the gods they had created, to the temples where those gods 'resided' and through receiving prasadams and temple honours, the landlord families of the vellala caste occupied a place next to the brahmins and above the other castes. Over time, traders and artisans who were in a lower position in the caste hierarchy moved up, by giving donations and grants to the temples. Puranic stories were spun and circulated that each of these castes originated from the holy fire of the yagna pit and from the god Indra and the moon. Till today the belief is that without the blessings of the brahmin and of the gods he has spawned, no caste can get status. For ceremonies like house-warming, or a wedding, a brahmin priest has to be present to chant the mantras. This belief is deep-seated. Treating such superstitious beliefs of the Hindus as a resource, brahmins gained ideological and economic control. Today, they and the Hindus of the next rung, hold the industrial capital of private enterprise next only to the government's capital. A number of cultivator castes now form the agricultural bourgeoisie. They are the wealthy kulaks in their respective areas. The bulk of the Hindus are the people between this stratum and dalits who are treated as untouchables. Referring to these people from a class perspective, Achin Vanaik calls them the 'agricultural bourgeoisie + rural side, urban petty bourgeoisie classes'.[2]

The Hindus who are between the two extremes are the active population in contemporary India. In Tamil Nadu these middle-level Hindus appear as the people who patronise the dominant Hindu culture created by the coalition between brahmins and vellalas. Most of the caste riots and communal flare-ups have occurred among these castes of the middle position. Achin Vanaik points out that these middle castes are the main social force behind Hindu fundamentalism and communalism that have been gaining ground since Independence.[3] Hindu communalism is a manifestation of a force that has been empowered and is growing. The voice of these forces does not echo the pleas of the oppressed people.

Hindu Communalism

Hindu culture launched by Brahminism is unable to bring under one banner rural and urban working classes and the immense number of people from the middle-level castes and the dalits immersed in the clan culture. It is also erasing the distinctions among the agricultural bourgeoisie and the petty bourgeoisie, who both nurture Hindu communalism. We observe that Hindu culture, its caste divisions and communalism, are the basic reason for the economically oppressed classes failing to organize themselves into a single group. Most of the riots and uprisings are a result of people attempting to move up in the brahminic caste hierarchy. All efforts by dalits and other low-caste people to move up economically and socially are seen by the middle-level castes as a challenge to their status.

Hindu Caste and the Dalit

To raise their status in the hierarchy, people from trader and artisan castes were keen on participating in worship in vedic temples, and in giving donations and votive offerings. A caste does not gain higher status by its economic condition alone. Recognition by vedic Brahminism is the criterion for improving one's caste status. The social dynamic in Indian society is very different from the West where economic position is the primary and the final norm that decides one's status. It is particularly difficult for dalits to transcend the social restrictions laid down by Hindu culture and attain a higher rank through economic improvement. Though now it is possible for a few dalits to acquire wealth through reservation, when it comes to ranking in caste terms there is no change. Therefore if one wants to move up in the caste hierarchy, one has to be associated with the brahminic temples that are replete with meaningless rituals and ceremonies. One has to get Sanskritized.

Some of the educated dalits are taking this trajectory, though this is possible only in an urban context. Most of the dalits affected by untouchability, insults, fear, hunger, disease, and ignorance are in the rural areas. They cannot get involved in the activities of vedic temples because the doors are still closed to them. Living and dying outside is their lot. Village deities, the gods of the dalits, are stigmatized by Hindu culture as being lower, cruel and evil. Even today some dalits are trying to raise their status a little by participating in the festivities of village temples. But that is not easy. Either they do not get any role or they are allotted a minor role on the last day of the festival. In some villages when the dalits ignore the restriction and try to participate, they face violence from the middle-level castes. In spite of innumerable atrocities there is an urge among dalits to get a foothold in the dominant caste culture. As long as they are in this mindset, there seems to be no other way/choice for them.

For vedic temple worship, the cooperation of the local castes is essential which in turn requires a framework of castes, the gods of the vedic brahmins and the priests. Dalits have no place in this framework. They are referred to as 'outcastes'. Nor can they gain a place there because dalits, in reality, are not within the ambit of Hindu culture. In the Hindu social structure you have only brahmins, kshatriyas, vellalas (known also as vaishyas) and shudras. Along with hill tribes and other tribes, dalits are beyond the pale of this formation. Dalits and hill tribes are not only suppressed and devastated by that culture but are in fact the indirect creation and result of it. The people inside the caste formation have been projected as normal people and dalits and tribals branded as deviants and marginals.

Dalits and Conversion

We have to bear in mind these facts while examining the efforts of dalits to convert. There was a time when Hindus ridiculed the conversion of dalits to Buddhism, Christianity and Islam as a step to gain a livelihood. But now, in independent India, they are agitated about the conversion of dalits. It is now obvious that their cry that dalits are in fact Hindus is only to defend Hindu majoritarianism and domination. This cry has been only heard since dalits began participating politically in the democratic government of the bourgeoisie. During British rule a large number of dalits converted to Christianity. But missionaries like Robert De Nobili and Constantine Beschi, who were converting people to Christianity in the seventeenth and eighteenth centuries, imitated the brahmins and changed the Christianity of equality into a Christianity of caste. They assumed brahminic sounding names like Thathuvapothakaswamy and Thairyanathar alias Veeramaamunivar, respectively, and led moral and exclusive lives and preached like brahmins. They lived in brahmin enclaves (*agraharams*), called themselves 'ayyar', sported a sacred thread, wore saffron cloth, sat on deer/tiger-hides, turned vegetarian and travelled in palanquins. They made Christianity into a caste-based religion. They expounded the Bible in a manner suitable to the brahmin-vellala combine. From the time of these two preachers, Catholicism in Tamil Nadu became a brahmin-vellala religion. The brahmins and vellalas who converted to Christianity, retained a Hindu caste ambience. They ensured that they got precedence and a place of honour in matters relating to the Church. Untouchability was extended to dalit Christians also. On the whole Christianity was comfortably accommodated within the ambit of the brahminic Hindu cultural formation.

No Liberation through Religions

It is clear that dalits cannot improve their status in the dominant Hindu-Christian culture through religion and worship. Their attempts to move ahead socially have been violently put down. From ancient times, dalits have been worshipping village deities to meet the socio-psychological needs of their community life. Even in this worship the place of honour is demanded by caste Hindus who dominate local land-ownership and caste hierarchies. In the village deity festivals conducted by dalits, upper-caste people claim precedence in receiving offerings like pongal and prasadam. This entitlement is used by them to re-inforce their domination over dalits.

In addition, dalits organize their patterns of worship along the lines of vedic temples, with similar rituals, icons, festivals and temple architecture to those of the hegemonic castes. Whenever dalits resort to these devices to elevate their status a little, this is looked upon as a challenge to upper-caste Hinduism. Many dalits get killed. Similarly when dalits try to use the village commons they are attacked.

Two Different Moralities/Moral Orders

The same dominant castes which claim that their culture is superior try to eliminate dalits if they ever try to follow that culture. Why this contradiction? The caste Hindu who declares that dalits are Hindus, locates them permanently outside the pale of caste. What do we learn from this? In reality they expect that dalits should forever remain suppressed and exist like cattle, completely ignored. There must be some deep-rooted reason for dominant Hindu, Christian, and Islamic castes to look down upon dalits and view them as lower than animals. There is not even an iota of moral anger or guilt on the part of any dominant Hindu caste on being the cause of the situation in which dalits encounter scarcity, injustice, cruelty and annihilation. They do not see anything wrong in this condition. They think that this is but natural. When dalits are oppressed the conscience of the upper castes is not in the least troubled.

It appears that the code of Hindu culture is that dalits should do hard manual labour; die in poverty; live only in huts; and live outside the village without any sanitation. They should do menial work for caste Hindus like slaves. Every Hindu believes that one is cursed to be born a dalit (like being born a woman) and that this is the result of sins in the previous birth. An upper-caste Hindu believes that he is born into his caste because of his good deeds in his earlier birth and God's grace. Even dalits accept this proposition. So, according to Hindu culture, it is believed there are two different moralities, one for dalits and the other for dominant castes.

A dalit is needed for the brahmin to believe that he is at the apex of the caste hierarchy, that he is utterly clean/pure, that the dalit who is at the root of the tree, along with mud, is completely unclean. So we see that one who is far removed from manual labour gets a high position, and one whose life is intertwined with labour is relegated to the lowest place. This is true not only for the Hindu casteist feudal culture but also for all cultures that are driven by class differences.

Two Different Identities

A negative identity for dalits has been created deep in the mind of the Hindu dominant castes. To them it comes naturally to think of themselves in terms of a positive identity and the dalits as having a negative identity. They are happy that they were not born dalits and simultaneously apprehensive that they might become like dalits. Whenever a dalit tries to uplift himself, a caste Hindu is anxious and agitated that he may be deprived of his own positive identity and that the negative identity of the upward moving dalit may reach him. This anxiety develops into a fury. The Hindu is unable to break out of this caste psychology. In the caste hierarchy, every upper-caste person approaches the one below him with a similar psychology. He is even prepared to make sacrifices for this. At all times he carries the burden of purity of caste and the fear that this state might be compromised by the lower castes. Coming together on the basis of economic position as a class is not as important as guarding his caste intact. The dominant landowning castes make sure that the middle-level castes in rural areas, lower castes and dalits who work as agricultural labourers, do not meet, unite or in any way organize themselves or transcend caste identities. The hegemonic castes often engender clashes between these groups to try to protect their own class interests. When many caste groups function amidst mutual hostilities they are unable to fuse under a single banner. Lewis Coser points out that revolutionary class struggle goes missing because of the conflicts among different castes in Hindu society.[4] Even among the different castes among dalits, and between dalits and other middle-level castes, clashes keep occurring. Instead of class struggle, encounters between different castes occur. Such encounters can never eradicate inequality. Nor can they demolish the caste structure. As Richard Lannoy argues, in fact these clashes strengthen inequality. They do not challenge the existing order.[5]

In many instances, it is dalits who get killed. Though the basic ideology of the caste system is provided by Brahminism, each caste in the hierarchy oppresses the group below in the caste order. Whenever dalits with the Hindu label try to elevate themselves within the Hindu culture, it is the middle-level castes that destroy the life and property of the dalits. The riots that took place in Puliangudi (2011), Mudukulathur (2011), Meenakshipuram (1997), Bodinayakanoor (2012) and Viluppuram (2013) confirm this. The middle-level castes believe that by imposing the degenerate brahminic ideology on dalits, they protect their own status. In 1930, the thevars of Ramanathapuram declared that dalits should not wear gold jewels, own anything, dress to cover themselves fully, get educated or develop self-respect. Here Ambedkar pointed out that there was little difference between these regulations and the laws of Manu. If one observes carefully, one sees that each caste has visibly/distinct recognizable indications of their status in dress, ornaments, and in the musical instruments played at their weddings. Beginning with the brahmins, each caste is keen on imposing such caste signs on those below them. In this respect each caste behaves like brahmins. Therefore you have the unusual situation of two dalit castes subjected to similar caste-based restrictions not identifying themselves as victims of related oppression. They would rather figure out which is superior to the other. They bond with the petty bourgeoisie among their own caste, or use their caste to elevate themselves to gain petty bourgeoisie status. Or betray their own caste folks to the landlords who control them.

Neo-Brahminism

Brahminism operates in such a way that dalits are caught in the hold of Hindu culture and are unable to develop their own economic and cultural life. In addition, in modern times, Brahminism has been acting behind the curtain called 'democracy' and double-dealing in the name of Western bourgeoisie ideology. Neo-Brahminism, through its propaganda, has convinced the oppressed people to get used to their condition. It continues its cultural aggression. For instance, Paulo Freire says the central problem is this:

> How can the oppressed, as divided inauthentic beings, participate in developing the pedagogy of their liberation? Only as they discover in themselves to be 'hosts' of the oppressor can they contribute to the midwifery of their liberating pedagogy. As long as they live in the duality in which *to be* is to be *like*, and *to be like* is *to be like the oppressor*, this contribution is impossible. The pedagogy of the oppressed is an instrument for their critical discovery that both they and their oppressor are manifestations of dehumanization.'[6]

The marginalized are manipulated to believe this. On the one side, runs this propaganda, while on the other it is believed that the same caste groups that branded dalits as untouchables would come forward and declare that something should be done to ameliorate their plight. They blame dalits for their condition, forgetting that they and their ancestors are responsible for the dalit predicament. They say that dalits have to change, not accepting that it is *they* who need to change their ways. Some of the educated, petty bourgeois dalits in the cities who consider themselves 'progressive' make the same mistake. These are the people who have internalized the ideology of neo-Brahminism and the democratic government and are gradually getting alienated from the majority of dalit people.

Whenever there is a threat to Brahminism from outside we hear the argument that there should be no caste discrimination, there is no inequality and that everyone is equal. When Jainism and Buddhism rose in revolt against the brahminical caste system, dalits like Kannappan and Nandan in Tamil Nadu were given the rubric Nayanmar (saivite saints). Brahminism began a self-defence act by saying whatever caste one belongs to if one practises piety one can attain deliverance. Later, in order to drive the white man away so that they could indulge in exploitation, brahmins and their allies raised the slogans like we are all Indians and are all children of Mother Bharath. Dalits should not forget that all this chicanery is only a protective mechanism of the dominant group. Once they consolidate authority in their hands, they inflict with greater vigour the ideology of inequity and physical violence on the working people.

One point is clear from the above observations. The caste formation of Hindus and Christians facilitates keeping the dalits as they are, marginalized. For each caste there are different rules of behaviour. There is no common code. If at all there is such a code, it only facilitates keeping the people at the base (like the dalits), forever enslaved. They do not have any moral, logical or the much publicized humanitarian basis to redeem dalits. And dalits should be aware of this.

Hinduism and the Dalit

In spite of all this, if dalits have any hankering for Hindu culture, if they crave moving up in the caste hierarchy, they should examine the place of a dalit in Hinduism. In brahminic Hinduism, the 'life' that is supposed to have been before and after the birth of a human is considered important. The present life is a reward or punishment for the life we led or our actions in the previous birth. This view explains the conflicts in human life between birth and death on the basis of what happened before birth. And the consequences will come after death. For whom is this view favourable? For the haves or for the have-nots? It is understandable that the have-not wants her or his life to be changed. Only those who have been subordinated and marginalized would like to have the social structure changed in order to elevate themselves. The one who is comfortable will be interested in maintaining the status quo, the social structure and its hegemonic hold. That is the reason why Hindu culture has developed into an arrangement to protect the welfare and authority of brahmins. Possible changes are placed prior to birth and after death. The cunning brain of the priestly class has laid down that in this life each one should perform his/her duties and meet his/her obligations meticulously. The codes of Hindu culture insist that the duty of the base-line working class of the dalit is to be a slave to all others and earn a livelihood by hard physical labour. They also ordain that dalits and women are a cursed lot, born because of sin. To be born a dalit is the result of a curse and so a dalit's whole life is cursed. His whole life is one of atonement. So if dalits are mutilated, burnt, their huts torched, their possessions scorched, their women molested, all these acts are looked upon as expiation for their sins. The very life of a dalit is a punishment. To live as unworthy of elementary social and economic rights is the atonement to ensure salvation.

When upper-caste people renounce and appear humble, simple, Hinduism describes this as a superior discipline.

But when one is born a dalit, without any possessions or rights, and is in dire poverty, it is said that this is a result of one's sin. One state occurring among two different castes is seen as two dissimilar conditions. The simplicity and austerity of Gandhi and Saint Appar, both of whom were from high castes, is acknowledged as the quality of great souls; but for the dalit who leads a cursed life this is seen as a retribution for his sins. In Hindu culture the same factor, which bestows honour, sanctity and respect and related authority on a member of the upper caste, inflicts sin and curse on a dalit.

In Bakthi literature, there are instances of Hindus from dominant castes such as Saints Appar and Sambandar and the dalit Nandan praying for deliverance. In their prayers we notice these two different approaches. Death for the high-caste Hindu is redemption; but for the dalit it is an escape from his lowly birth. Hinduism which has made the dalits children of sin has also created the concept of pollution to justify this. In this pollution code laid down by the brahmins, working-class dalits, are the equals of objects and animals and seen as pollutants. In the hierarchy of Hindu castes, a dalit can only be an untouchable sinner. He cannot be a human being. Nowhere else in the world can one witness such injustice. Even the respect extended to a cow is not given to a dalit. Brahminism which suggests ways of neutralizing pollution for a caste Hindu, instructs a dalit to live as an untouchable. And that is his atonement. A dalit cannot be rid of pollution till death. Even after he dies, it sticks, through his descendents. After all, a dalit can only marry within his caste. Though the Hindu woman is also a cursed being becoming untouchable during menstruation and at childbirth, after these are over she can return to society following purification ceremonies. A dalit however remains polluted forever.

II

Dalit Culture

On more than one occasion Ambedkar pointed out that dalits are not Hindus and that they were excluded.[7] He battled with Gandhi at the Round Table Conference over this issue. If that is so, is there such a thing as dalit culture? How should that culture be organized? What is the role of the upsurge of dalit culture, in the governmental, capitalist, socio-economic structure? Is it proper for dalits, according to the present constitution of the Indian government, to accept the quota reserved in the name of religion and caste? Is it all right for them to seek a role in temple worship, involve themselves in politics, find a place in the bureaucracy and team up with capitalists? Questions such as these are inevitable both from dalits and from those opposed to dalits. It can be observed that these questions are about the place of dalit culture in the Indian multi-cultural, class and national ethos. These questions are also about the position of the dalit struggle in the social movement against the Indian capitalistic and agricultural framework.

Dalit Protest-Culture: The First Stage

Clearly dalits are in a situation in which they have to organize their own liberation so the liberation movement that they design should have two dimensions. Firstly, cutting through nationality, race and language, dalit culture should identify with other people similarly discriminated at birth, due to the colour of their skin like the blacks, or due to gender like women. In addition to this, in India there are other people like them who cannot be considered of Indian nationality but are of a subservient position. These are the hill folks

and other tribes. Dalits should join them and construct a distinct sub-national culture, different from that of the other
nationalisms. The dalit sub-national culture thus created will
have much in common with that of the black and Feminist
movements. Such a dalit culture is bound to be a protest
culture. With the rise of this culture of protest, dalits can
jettison the brahminical-Hindu casteist garbage they have
accumulated over millennia. Then the importance hitherto
denied to the working class can be redeemed. The hegemonic class, to further their own interests, has loaded dalits
with a certain ideological burden. Their protest culture
should instil enough courage among dalits to disown this
load and discard it. This is easier to talk and write about than
to carry out. Dalits steeped in guilt, fear, despair, poverty,
centuries of ignorance, slave mentality and apprehension
of change, will find it difficult to free themselves from this
mindset. Only by ignoring, attacking, humiliating, rejecting
and ridiculing this hegemonic culture and its symbols step
by step, can dalits get rid of their mental blocks. Dalit protest
culture can do all these though superficially it may appear
like a mere anarchist culture. Brahminical culture took the
form of Hindu culture, a poisonous set of mores with the sole
aim of protecting the landownership interests of the hegemonic castes. To do this, the people were fitted into a maze
of social, economic and cultural relationships through the
caste framework. Government, caste, religion, gods, code of
conduct, ethics, justice, rules governing man-woman relationships, ideology of family, literature . . . all these were created
so that the people in this structure of social and economic
relationships might believe that it had been constructed for
their benefit.

Though this construct appears to be common to all Hindus,
for working-class dalits, it has a different face. Justice, ethics,
codes of conduct, God, dharma, literature are designed to be
more supportive of the brahmins, and according to the caste
hierarchy gradually less and less supportive as one comes to
dalits. According to the laws of Manu, with dalits, issues like

justice are seen as reduced, degraded and despicable. It can be seen clearly that according to Hindu-brahmin culture, dalits are viewed as anarchists. But in fact dalits can be called rebels. The hegemonic group fears the untouchable dalits, wondering what form their protest will assume. Only when dalits transform themselves into protestors, as feared by the upper castes, can we say that the first stage of dalit liberation has begun. Dalit weapons of protest can be found in the very culture that oppresses them.

The Counter Culture

We already have an alternate cultural tradition among the marginalized tribal people, hill people, who have been living at the edge of history, and among dalits who are in fact partly tribal. This can provide the impetus needed for the first step in setting up a dalit protest culture. In fact, elements of this alternate culture are visible even among oppressed women. It can be discerned among all the marginalized people subjected to oppression. Richard Lannoy called this antipodal culture. It can also be termed the 'other culture'. Lannoy points out that this antipodal culture functions diametrically opposite to the hegemonic order. He goes on to describe the characteristics of these two cultures.

> The hegemonic culture which emphasizes order, obedience to rules and regulations, stresses the differences and distinctions, adheres to the taboos, living strictly with the reality principle, living a measured and careful life, encouraging rivalry among caste groups.[8]

At the same time, in the antipodal culture that is outside the hegemonic one, we notice the following features that are opposed to the above:

> Live as per an irrational motivation,
> Always transcend differences and move towards unity,

Skip taboos,
Live an Epicurean life, a life of pleasure,
Unrestricted enjoyment and celebration of community life.[9]

Cultural anthropologists have pointed out that these antipodal cultural features are clearly discernible among oppressed
people such as dalits, women and tribal people. In communities where the division of labour, the ownership of property,
and individualistic behaviour related to these are less marked,
antipodal culture can be observed. During community
worship and festivals, hedonistic behaviour and violations
of normal mores are seen among most of these people.
Ranajit Guha points out that rebellion against the British
East India Company and their allies, the local landlords, by
the Santhal and Munda tribes, usually began during their
festivals.[10] In the villages of Tamil Nadu, today caste clashes
are sparked off during festivals. In animal sacrifices and
rituals, dalits and related caste people, and women get pos-
sessed, go into trances and act as oracles. This is nothing but
an expression of the features of deep rooted protest culture
in them.

Lannoy points out that there are some common cultural
features between tribal people and the untouchables who
are violently marginalized in brahminical Hindu society:

In common with Hindu lower castes, the tribes/tribals
emphasize equality in social behaviour within the ethnic
group, greater equality of status for women, more liberal
relations between the sexes (men and women work
together), a more personal relationship between husband
and wife, a more 'romantic' type of courtship, love adven-
tures and love feuds, and, as would be expected, a greater
emphasis on self-reliance in child care. Pollution rules are
far more relaxed among tribals than among castes. The
absence of puritanism, frank indulgence in pleasure, and
a strong sense of communal identity all favour the tribal
passion for music and dance at which many excel.[11]

All of this fits into the characteristics of the antipodal culture described earlier. Among educated dalits who have moved into the cities, these characteristics of positive counter culture are slowly disappearing because of the influence of the individualistic ideology of the West, and negatively due to brahminical Hindu culture. Though this counter culture has roots deep in the subconscious mind, many living in urban areas consider its features 'rustic and uncivilized' and deliberately try to hide them. When they visit villages these people consider this counter culture backward and unrefined and despise the dalits who live by them.

A Great Change (Inversion)

We have seen, how, among dalits, there are communal singers and women who are living in the protest culture or counter culture. This can be used to give initial momentum to the protest movement. We will have to examine what methods should be followed to generate protest culture and make it a part of the subconscious mind of dalits. In this context we have to recall some of the devices to be used in the first stage of the protest culture. Dr. Ambedkar listed inter-caste marriage, education, protest, destroying the Hindu Sastras and conversion as such devices. He asked if any dalit could respect Manu's law which labels him untouchable and says that he is not even human. Ambedkar persuaded dalits to burn copies of those Hindu laws. He himself burnt them.[12] Periyar also chose this pioneering mode of protest. Periyar pointed out that unless Hinduism and related religions were demolished, there would be no end to untouchability or caste. It has been emphasized that the culture of the oppressed is diametrically opposed to that of the hegemonic group. Merely by contemplating dalits cannot liberate themselves from the dominant culture that has turned them into upside down peoples of negative identity. We are not talking about the liberation of an individual. We are talking about the collective liberation of a people who have been suppressed as a community. So the protest culture of dalits will have to be totally new. When dalits project their culture this way, it will appear criminal, anarchist and rebellious. Let it be so. It should appear so. Long ago, Periyar pointed out that only if it appears rebellious would it indicate that the suppressed are active.

> If this is criminal, if this is sinful, then each one of us can jolly well commit this crime, this sin.[13]

This statement is so very appropriate to the context of dalit protest culture.

Only in the form of counter culture can the dalit movement participate in the liberation of humanity. Often in history the suppressed spawn violence. But people such as dalits are victims and not perpetrators of violence. Each attempt of dalits to escape from the hold of their suppressers is seen as violence and rebellion. The oppressor will describe the dalit as a rogue, barbaric, rowdy and a terrorist. What the accused said in the case of burning forty-three dalits alive in Venmani village proves this.

> Earlier these coolies used to work hard, were respectful. They came and stood in the backyard. Now, influenced by Communists, they appear and stand on the verandah with their footwear on. They talk with us face to face, on equal terms. They have grown lazy and arrogant.' – Indira Parathasarathy, *Kuruthi Punal*

It can be seen that if dalit people wear chappals, stand on the verandah, and speak on equal terms, that itself is considered a deep insult to upper castes. One dimension of the dalit protest culture is to pull off an inversion. It should attack the 'sacred', prestigious, cultural symbols that help brahminical Hindu culture retain its hegemonic hold. If we are to break the dominance-slave/master-slave order, we have to despise and discard the ideological symbols that brought about such a framework. If the dalit adopts such symbols it would mean that he accepts this dominance-slave order. By accepting that order can the slave become the dominant one? A worker may become the factory owner or a poor man, a wealthy man. But can a dalit become a brahmin? He cannot because here the dominant servile order is decided by birth. Remember that it does not change even in and after death.

It is not our aim to become a capitalist, a rich man or a brahmin. To grow into a capitalist one needs a number of workers. Similarly to become a wealthy person, there must be a lot of poor people. To become a brahmin, you need to have a whole hierarchy of lower castes below you. That is the reason why we reject the whole dominant-slave order. Only when dalit protest culture destroys and discards this loathsome order can people realize that they need be neither a crypto brahmin nor a dalit but live as human beings. When we talk about human beings it is not about abstract, absolute humans. We do not refer to those people who are supposed to have some sacred 'humanness' within them. Those who are not identified by either dominance or slavery are referred to here as 'human'.

These protests (by the dalits) have created panic among the guardians of hegemonic culture. The Puranas predict that at the end of Kaliyuga the despicable shudras, would invert the cultural symbols of the other three varnas and appropriate them as their own. When Kaliyuga concludes, the brahmin will turn into shudra, the shudra will morph into brahmin, the king like the thief and the thief like the king. Inversion will change everything; *Vayupurana* laments that wives will not be faithful to their husbands and servants will refuse to obey their masters.[14] In Christian mythology also we can see prophecies about such upside down changes in the context of the appearance of the Anti-Christ during doomsday. It has been pointed out earlier that the dominant person has attributed a positive identity to himself and a negative identity to the oppressed. In the dalit protest cultural movement, these identities are shaken. For those who are dominating, these changes appear anarchic and dangerous. On the other hand, for the dalit they augur equality, social harmony, happiness, and the freedom that arises out of a property-less situation.

The Signs of a Dominance-Slavery Relationship

In the hegemonic culture a number of signs have been developed to indicate the state of slavery.

On the basis of semiotics, Ranajit Guha elaborately explains that these signs depend on language, writing, gesture and place. When a dalit talks with someone from a superior caste, he is expected to degrade and debase himself. He should discount the house he lives in, his food, his status and all that is related to him. Often he will have to remain quiet without uttering a word. There should be no back chat. These are some of the regulations of language imposed on the dalit by the hegemonic culture. If a dalit ignores these restrictions even slightly, the dominant person will be outraged and brand him as arrogant and disrespectful. When a dalit talks back, the positive and negative identities change places. Though the dalit gets relief from restrictions that bind him, the upper-caste man is indignant that his positive identities are lost. No dominant person would like to lose his identifiers.

Dalits should not adhere to these language regulations. They should not be silent. They should not keep their mouths shut. There is no need to degrade yourself. Talk! Keep talking! Speak up loudly! Speak in your Tamil. Speak in your language that has been despised as *cheri* Tamil and colloquial Tamil! Transgress the elitist order of language laid down by 'superior culture'. The niceties prescribed in handling certain words as euphemisms and politeness should be violated.

Education and Literacy

Similarly, education and literacy have been symbols of dominance. When dalit agricultural workers in rural areas send their children to school, they are discouraged by the dominant castes. 'What is he going to achieve by studying? Let him learn to graze the cattle properly.' This can be observed even today. If a dalit talks back this is referred to as a pernicious outcome of education. Hindu Sastras persuade them not to go to school but toil in the field and slog as slaves. Will not the whole paradigm of positive identity and negative identity reverse if dalits get educated? Did not Manu lay down that if any dalit reads or even listens to the Vedas, his limbs should be mutilated? Realizing this Ambedkar gave prime place to 'study' in the scheme of things he prescribed for dalits. In the protest culture of dalits, education is one of the techniques of inversion.

Body Language

In the same way, body language, gestures, measures of time and place all act as signs that distinguish the oppressed state of dalits. In the pre-literacy era, each community utilized the human body as a site to preserve and protect the fundamentals of its culture. In those times there was no other instrument of recording than the body. The Hindu Sastras detail the signs that have been documented in the body. Manu has listed actions such as standing up when someone enters/approaches, wrapping the shoulder around the waist, touching the feet and prostrating, as the bodily gestures that symbolize an enslaved and lowly position. This also applies to women. It has been stated that the above bodily gestures should be used by the son to the father, the wife to the husband, the slave to the master, the low caste to the upper caste, a disciple to his guru and a devotee to god to establish their lowly and subjective state.

Dalits should defy and discard these rules. Do not fall at anyone's feet. Do not tie your upper cloth around the waist. Do not stand with your arms across your chest. Do not bend. Do not bow your head; you should stand firm, straight, chest thrust forward; do not keep a respectful distance from the upper-caste man. You should not take up residence away from the village. Similarly, dalits should start using aluminium or stainless vessels instead of earthenware vessels. Discard your pots of clay not because these are stigmatized but because the upper-caste people insist that dalits should use only mud vessels. In other words, whatever is attributed to dalits as theirs and whenever it is expected of them to follow certain practices to establish their slave status, those very practices should be eschewed diligently.

Action According to Context

Though poverty, starvation, ignorance and unemployment are common in all the villages of India, the hierarchy of caste structure and related cultural variations differ from village to village. This is because the features of hegemonic culture that support slavish conditions can differ according to the nature of the place such as dry land and wet land. In a village, rules laid down by the upper caste might include that dalits can eat beef and drink arrack, as part of their despicable life style. In such a situation dalit people should eschew beef and liquor as a part of the protest culture strategy that aims at reversing the paradigms. But you may not be able to follow the same strategy in another place where the order of dominance is different. For economic reasons, or to shock the dominant caste or because there dalits live in a majority, dalits can eat beef, drink arrack. What is important here is to see that we as dalits carry out these actions consciously as a part of our protest culture.

When dalits construct their protest culture in this manner, they have necessarily to operate within the cultural ambiance of the opponent group. There is no other way. They have to select their weapons from the very hegemonic order against which they have been compelled to protest. As a part of the struggle, dalits have to participate in Hinduism, caste, and Hinduized-Christian worship. It is true that dalits are not Hindus. They are outside the pale of caste. Even so, they have to carry out their protest using caste and religion as media. Some people may label this opportunism. They will point out that this is not an honest approach. Our answer to this criticism should be that we do not need such honesty, ethics, justice, dharma or any such rubbish. Our idea in touching upon issues like Hinduism, Hinduized Christianity, caste, temple entry, right to worship, right to become a priest, is only to obliterate them. We follow these strategies to take dalit protest culture forward as a movement and through that path enable ourselves and our descendants to stand erect as human beings. In dalit history, whenever there have been clashes in rural areas, lower castes who opposed upper castes desisted from killing them. It was not out of compassion. The low castes are caught in the brahminic-Hindu cultural mesh spread by the upper caste and are therefore just too weak to get up.

Dalit Protest-Culture: The Second Stage

The inverted actions taken as a part of dalit protest culture are admirable cultural activities. It is unfair to label them as wrong. Individual delinquency is perpetrated by the chicanery of a few or groups with private gain in mind. But dalit protest is a public, social happening. It is an outward cultural expression of affected people. It is this happening which prepares dalits for the second stage of revolutionary action. The rise of dalit protest culture has to take place before the socialist, Communist revolution called class struggle anticipated by Marxism. Only then can the compromises and casteist approaches of the Indian Communist movement disappear. Dalit protest culture is the first stage in this path of revolution. At the same time, as Paulo Freire cautions, while we conduct a struggle against the national bourgeois class, there is chance that an illusory path will appear. Some dalit leaders may betray the movement by getting close to and negotiating with the dominant castes, capitalists and kulaks. Our leaders may become puppets in their hands. Such leaders will be part of the rural petty bourgeoisie or urban petty bourgeoisie. For personal gain, they will align with parties that play vote bank politics or communist parties that are ready to compromise. The dominant class creates such people among the dalits. Paulo Freire labelled these leaders amphibians, like frogs, who act as brokers between dalits and the dominant class.[15]

Dalits are not denigrated on an individual basis as wicked and malevolent. They are considered collectively polluting, sinful beings who are kept outside the pale of caste on the basis of their birth. So for them deliverance cannot be on an individual basis. Some educated dalits think that they can escape the stigma of being dalit by brahminizing; they become victims of capitalist cultural aggression. Individual dalit liberation is an impossibility. One can hide facts and live but that would be a sham. Only when you lead an open life can there be guiltless happiness. If someone believes that he/she can get deliverance individually, that can only be an escape and a delusion. It is not deliverance; it is an attempt to join the dominant forces. A people who have been collectively marginalized, can attain liberation only by combined struggle. Liberation is a state without domination, slavery and negative identities.

Developing Self-Confidence among Dalits

Dalits, particularly those in villages who on a daily basis encounter oppression will not easily come forward to reverse the symbols of hegemony and slavery. They are languishing without any self-confidence. Even the thought of opposing the upper castes makes them afraid. They are likely to be subjected to physical violence at any time. It is well known that the police, in the name of a democratic government, acts as defenders of caste Hindus against dalits. They behave like agents of an anti-democratic force. The Indian army, the paramilitary forces and armed police under the state government will not hesitate to charge against the urban working class and rural agricultural labourers, mostly dalits. In this situation, it is understandable that dalits fear for their lives and possessions.

Publicizing the Limitations of the Enemy

What should not be forgotten is that our oppressors are not extraordinary people. They are a bundle of weaknesses and fears. Dalits should realize this. Protest culture will bring about this understanding. To develop self-confidence among dalits, the meanness and malice of the upper castes should be exposed. In addition, the skill and growth of the new generation of dalits should be publicized. The dishonourable conduct of hegemonic leaders who sport haloes with the rubrics such as godmen, religious heads, and bishops should be explained with a view to nursing the self-confidence of young dalits.

The Catholic priest Dubois documented the 'wicked' activities of the brahmins who lived in nineteenth-century Tamil Nadu. According to him, a brahmin child does not display any respect or admiration for other human beings. But malevolence and vendetta are found generation after generation among brahmins and upper-caste Hindus. Though Lawgiver Manu boasted that these people had peaceful, regal qualities, that was far from the truth. Black magic is a favourite way of a brahmin wreaking vengeance. His main weapon is false accusation against his enemy. A brahmin grows up as a selfish human being. At the slightest provocation he will betray the cause of the country. He believes that he is superior to everyone and so despises all others. He believes that there is no place in his life for gratitude, compassion and concern for others. He is answerable only to his own caste folks. From his birth he is taught that everyone else is lower than him. He thinks that others should do chores and meet his needs. It must be publicized among dalits that Hindu culture with this kind of anti-human being orientation cannot in any way be just.[16]

In addition to this, the achievements of young dalit men and women who in a single generation have overtaken those in the upper caste should be made known. Above all, they should know about the dalit leader of India, Dr. Ambedkar. His knowledge, political sagacity, penchant for struggle, erudition and sharpness of intellect should be made known to the younger generation. The traditional performing arts of the dalits, such as *koothu paattu* (song) and group dances should be nurtured and shown to the world. All these steps would help build up the self-confidence of dalits. It will not pave the way for dalit dominance as some seem to fear. Unlike the upper- and middle-level castes, dalits are not fighting to get authority. Their fight is to destroy dominance. Only in the obliteration of dominance, for dalits and for all other humans, is there a future.

Revolutionary Struggle and Politics

Dalit protest culture cannot forever be operating on one plane, inverting the symbols of hegemonic culture. If it does then there is the danger of moving towards revivalism. Opposing something for the sake of protest can become a meaningless ritual. Being short of subnational identity, the dalits who are protesting against discriminations are not floating in the air. They are tied up with a nation and its fate. The nation in turn is connected to the whole world. The basic power structure of India, beginning with foreign investment, through internal private capital rests with governmental investments. Dalits, along with some other middle-level and lower castes, bear the burden of the authority of the capitalist class. Only when they take part in socialist revolutionary politics and ensure final economic equality, can they realize economic, social, cultural and political liberation. In this process they will have to oppose capitalists, the landowning bourgeoisie and lumpen classes that live off them.

To put it simply, dalit struggle that begins as a protest movement in the cultural plane should gradually assume the dimensions of a struggle for human liberation. In this struggle, dalits will join middle-, lower- and upper-level castes and everyone will give up their caste identities, and assume class identities if at all this is feasible. Dalit protest culture will help erase the religious and caste identities of the middle and lower castes who are held together by economic and cultural oppression. However, what is to be borne in mind is that the aim is not to become a brahmin or a vellala or any other caste but to be a human being.

Scientific Assessment

The origins of the symbols and signs of hegemony need to be scientifically analysed; how the symbols and signs of hegemony came into being during the historical period. The argument of dalits should not be accepted at an emotional level as such an assessment can vary from person to person. We have to examine on a scientific basis the validity of the dalit voice in the present times. Is it valid, sound and legitimate? It is only then that at least some people from the upper strata will accept the stand of dalits. Such exceptions keep appearing, considering themselves dalits and being able to acquire a dalit perspective. Brahminic, hegemonic Hindu culture is anti-human. It is an established fact that it divides humans into different clusters. The Dalit Liberation movement should acquire the clout to convince even those in the dominant group that the Hindu culture makes humans decadent and appreciate that this is not a selfish dalit point of view. It is an objective fact.

Sathapathapiramanam I I 2.2.6; IV. 3.4.4.

Notes

1 Chandogya Upanishad, I 12. 1–5.
2 Achin Vanaik, *The Painful Transition: Bourgeois Democracy in India* (London: Verso, 1990).
3 Ibid.
4 Lewis Coser, *Sociology through Literature* (Englefield Hills, NJ: Prentice Hall, 1965).
5 Richard Lannoy. *The Speaking Tree: Study of Indian Culture and Society* (Oxford: Oxford University Press, 1971).
6 Paulo Freire, *Pedagogy of the Oppressed* (Harmondsworth: Penguin, 1973): 30.
7 Vasant Moon, ed., *Babasaheb Ambedkar :Writings and Speeches*, 22 vols. (Bombay: Government of Maharashtra, Department of Education, 1982).
8 Lannoy, *The Speaking Tree.*
9 Ibid.
10 Ranajit Guha, *Elementary Aspects of Peasant Insurgency in Colonial India* (Delhi: Oxford University Press, 1983).
11 Lannoy, *The Speaking Tree.*
12 V Moon, ed: *Babasaheb Ambedkar, Writings and Speeches.*
13 Anaimuthu. V, *Periyar E.V.R., Cintanaikal* (Trichi: Kazhagam, 1974).
14 Burton Stein, Burton. *Peasant State and Society in Medieval South India* (New Delhi: Oxford University Press, 1985); Indra Deva and Srirama Deva. *Traditional Values and Institutions in Indian Society* (New Delhi: Chand and Chand 1986).
15 Freire, *Pedagogy of the Oppressed.*
16 Abbé Jean Antoine Dubois, *Hindu Manners, Customs and Ceremonies* (New Delhi: Oxford University Press, 1982).

3

Periyapuranam:
Hierarchy and Inversion

Sekkizhar and Periyapuranam

It is said that *Periyapuranam* (The Great Purana) was written by Arulmozhithevar of the Sekkizhar clan of the vellala caste, about 800 years ago during the reign of the Chola king Kulothunga II (AD. 1133–50). *Periyapuranam* strings together the puranic life stories of some important and not-so-important individuals involved in the Saivite Bakthi of Siva. The first biographical work we Tamils are fortunate to have is *Periyapuranam!*

Arulmozhithevar, popularly known as Sekkizhar, was an important minister in the court of a Chola king. He owned land in immense proportions. He built a temple for Siva in his native village and endowed it with land so that it could benefit from a regular income. He was a representative of the community which dominated the central part of the Chola and Thondaimandalam region in the Tamil country. The community enjoyed all the rights over this area and the king established his sovereignty over these parts in a ritualistic manner. The nattars (local chiefs) of big and small territories that were within his realm exercised direct control over their subjects. Brahmin priests who inhabited the Sathur Vedhimangalam and Bramhadeya villages and temples affirmed the right of these hegemonic groups to lord it over the

49

people. This period can be best described as the Golden Age of the Hindu brahmin-vellalas. The story is not very different today.[1]

I

The god Siva is credited with three eyes. The puranic scribes equate them to the sun, the moon and fire. They also say that *Periyapuranam* is like the sun, *Thiruvilayadalpuranam* (episodes of Siva's interventions in the life of devotees) is like the moon and *Kandhapuranam,* which is about the life of Subramanian, one of the two sons of Siva, is like fire. Most of the Saivite saints about whom Sekkizhar gathered material belong to AD sixth to the ninth centuries, in other words, the Pallava and Pandya periods of South Indian history. These Pallavas were not of Tamil stock.[2] They were a powerful tribe from southern parts of India and were responsible for certain new movements in the Tamil country. There are some inscriptions that refer to them as 'those who cleared forests'. They cleared the jungle in the Thondaimandalam area and extended agricultural tracts.[3] During this period, some of the tribes and semi-tribes in the mountainous area and highlands also began to develop agricultural practices. In the process many of them were absorbed into the Hindu caste–religious system. The Pallava royal families called themselves kshatriyas and in turn they patronized the brahmins. The king was brahminized, meaning that he was accepted by the brahmins. He needed the temples, Saivite and Vaishnavite, along with the priests and sacred fires to legitimize his sovereignty over the people and the land. Fertile and productive paddy fields were donated to the brahmins who facilitated this process through the rituals in which they officiated.

It was during the Pallava days that Saivism took the Tamil country by storm. It was an emotional movement. A high degree of ecstasy and frenzy was evident. Song and dance were dominant. The elation and celebrations were not part

of the original brahminic way of worship. These features
were from tribal worship rituals and from the veneration of
the female deities of the rural subalterns. These developments have to be seen along with the advent of the Pallavas
and the involvement of tribal people in agriculture. It is
the passion of these tribal people that formed the basis of the
Bakthi movement. Its momentum transcended caste barriers. The Sanskritic-brahminical concept of pollution was
discarded through the story of the hunter Kannappan, narrated in *Periyapuranam*. The Bakthi movement was resilient
and generous. Utilizing this force, the agricultural clans and
landlords brought the urban traders under their control. It
was this interaction that was behind the struggle between
Saivism which was vedic and Jainism which was non-vedic.
But later, after the tenth century during the period of the
imperial Chola kings which was completely brahminized,
the Bakthi movement petered out and social formations
rigidified. Finally the society firmed up by brahminic ideology took the form of Hindu casteist society. The power over
people went into the hands of vellala–brahmin leaders. It was
at this period that *Periyapuranam* appeared.

From those days till today in Hindu society whenever
forces from the marginal areas, the landed areas and the
hill areas meet, there is turmoil followed by disintegration,
destruction and the appearance of a new hierarchical order.
This dynamic has been repeating itself over time. When the
wave of the Bakthi movement that affected the Tamil country
spread to the northern part of India during the eleventh
century, thanks to the work of Vaishnavite saint Ramanujar,
it created similar undercurrents. In Sikhism also one can
observe the hierarchical caste system. In Karnataka, the
Lingayats secured a high position in the order. Caste rigidity
in Hindu society loosened slightly. Much later, during the
emotional involvement of people in the freedom struggle,
after the advent of 'our own' rule, caste-religious formations
rigidified to control the new centres of power.

What is to be understood from these developments? In Hindu society change is permitted only within the given structure. Brahmins and those upper castes who managed to gain hegemony over the working-class castes will never tolerate any alteration in this structure. Max Weber has rightly said that 'Before everything else, without caste there is no Hindu'.[4] This is not only a historical truth but for a Hindu it is also a personal, distinct and psychological reality. *Periyapuranam* talks about these truths without any attempt at hiding them.[5] Sekkhizhar accepted Brahminism fully in the Saiva-vellalas age of the *Periyapuranam*.

We apply this to the Saivites who joined the anti-brahmin movement at the turn of the twentieth century. During that period, vedic religion that had been nurtured by the Bakthi movement was suitable for an agricultural society. The landlords of that society, Udayars, landowning castes, imposed their hegemony on the lower-caste people toiling in the fields. The social structure based on the brahminic caste edifice was designed appropriately to make the landlords feel that they were entitled to the service of this working class. It was advantageous for the brahmins as well as the landowning vellalas to make the working class believe that in this birth, it was only through physical labour that one could work out one's karma. This helped to keep them eternally at the base of the social, economic and political structure as low castes. For providing them with this device for exploitation, the vellala landlords gave the brahmin priests vast tracts of wetland under different categories such as *akarabrahmadeyam, Devathanam, Chathurvedhimangalam, pattaviruthi, suroththiriyam, aththiyayana viruththimaniyam, sarvamaniyam, ekapogam, kanapogam,* and so on. In return the brahmin priests gave the royal families Sanskrit titles such as *chakravarthi* and *thirubuvana chakravarthi*. They raised sacred fires in the temples and conducted yagnas and round-the-clock pujas. They attributed vedic origins to the vellala castes. For these castes the brahmin priests provided prime honour in the temples which exalted them in the eyes of the field hands. We observe that the brahmins are endowed with power only by brahminic Hinduism and that only by accepting their ideology do the landowning vellalas get economic and caste power. That is the reason why Periyar went on to say that only by demolishing Hindu religion can you destroy the hegemony of the brahmins.

Periyapuranam has to be seen against this backdrop. All the Saivite saints featured in this work are referred to with their caste identities. Then and now it is caste which is the unit of identification. The Saivite individuals mentioned in the text are of different castes based on the vocation they pursue such as brahmin, vellala, trader, king, artisan, hunter and pulaiyar. This classification is different from the four-fold (varna) northern set up of brahmins, kshatriyas, vaishyas and shudras. Here we commonly see the division as brahmins, shudras and those outside the pale of the caste system. The kings of the South are not connected with the kshatriyas of the North (such as Rajputs). In the Tamil country of ancient times, the kshatriya obligation to do battle was not taken on by any exclusive caste. Trained soldiers from different shudra castes like vellalas, barbers and maravars, formed the army. Similarly, unlike in the North where the baniyas formed the trading caste, here trading was done by people from different castes. Depending on the 'cleanliness' of the merchandise they handled, they took their place in the caste hierarchy. In the North, shudras are menials. But here some kammala castes and 'untouchable' castes are engaged in lowly chores. Here the vellala Hindus are not termed shudras. In the eyes of the brahmins in kaliyuga all those who are below them are shudras!

There are three leading figures in the Saivite Bakthi movement that *Periyapuranam* talks about: Sambandar, Appar and Sundarar. Appar is a vellala and the other two are brahmins. All three composed hymns, collectively titled *Thevaram,* in praise of Saivite temples. Like them, the Chera king Perumal and poet Punithavathi (Karaikal Ammaiyar) from the trading community also wrote devotional poems. Thirumoolar, born in the shepherd community, became a siddhar, a mystic, and wrote poems denying the existence of caste. There is no record of other Nayanmars (Saivite saints) writing devotional songs. They were busy doing the calling of their caste through which they showed their devotion. In his list of Nayanmars Sekkizhar has not included poets from the earlier centuries who wrote Saivite devotional literature. All the Nayanmars listed in *Periyapuranam* are from the Pallava era. We can conclude that the leading figures in this text are those who lived in the days of the Bakthi movement and later during the ninth to twelfth centuries. They were made puranic figures by Brahminism. By placing them in the hierarchy of Hindu social tradition and by analysing through the concept of inversion their devotional actions, we can understand them better.

II

The Hierarchy

Hierarchy is what we usually refer to as ordered inequality. However in the Hindu tradition there is a special connotation for this concept. In this hierarchy, not just human beings, but all connected things like articles, work, language, place, colour of skin, dress, habitat, gods, age, gender, body, animals, food and direction get an 'above' or 'below' place in the scheme of things. The pollution concept is also based on this scheme. Here cleanliness does not stop at the level of hygiene. We have to observe that it goes beyond; clean and dirty things are ritualistically associated with karma, birth, caste and redemption. According to this scale, brahmins are at the height of cleanliness and 'untouchables' are the lowest in filth; all the others occupy positions in between. The cow is the cleanest and dogs and pigs are the filthiest. In the *Panchakomya* (a concoction used in organic farming, prepared by mixing five products of the cow) milk is the cleanest while dung is the dirtiest. However, when compared with the untouchables, cow dung is considered clean. Where food is concerned, vegetables are clean while beef is contaminated. The human body is considered on the basis of this clean-unclean divide. The hierarchy of the clean unclean formation begins with the human body. The portion below the waist and the parts thereof, the orifices in that area, the excrescence from those vents, are considered dirty and therefore inferior. The upper portion of the body, particularly the head, is considered superior. Therefore in the Vedas, in 'Purusha Suktham' it is said that brahmins-kshatriyas are from the portion above the waist and the others came from the lower portion of the male body. We have to note that there is no birthplace for women and the vast number of people who are not shudras. Maybe that is the reason why much later, women were given the status of deities, and much later, untouchables were referred to as children of God! (Gandhi called the untouchables *harijans*, meaning children of God.)

This 'cleanliness' is injected into the soul. After it is completely cleansed and reaches the height of purity, the soul reaches 'mukthi' status. In that condition brahmins are in the first row, twirling their sacred threads. Since the souls of the other folks have not been thus cleansed, they take many births, in different castes. They get cleansed by fulfilling the obligations of the respective caste and then attain the twice-born status of the brahmins to reach the completely purified position. Relative purity has been made the basis for the Hindu hierarchical social structure while absolute purity has been made the basis for the liberation of the soul.[6] It can be seen that the brahminic priesthood, in order to gain advantage for its status, has tied up a matter that is basically in the realm of hygiene with spiritual issues. The combination of racial and ritual purities make vedic absolute purity.

The hegemonic group which has gained power on the basis of possession and rights has conceived this concept of cleanliness to stabilize its dominance by keeping the toiling masses under them. The idea behind this concept of cleanliness is to keep the working people perpetually under the control of the hegemonic group. In other words, class differences and methods of exploitation achieve legitimacy in terms of religion and have a place in the sub-conscious mind of a Hindu. Right from childhood, a Hindu is culturally moulded by language to look at everything as clean and unclean. Therefore a Hindu is not able to eat in another's home. He is not able to marry a woman from a different caste, particularly from a 'less clean' class. (But in a brahmin's relations with a sex worker then the 'cleanliness' aspect does not operate.) At the subconscious level clean-unclean construct is sometimes broken on the economic plane.

On the cultural plane, unless there is agitation and destruction by the 'unclean' people, unless there is an inversion that brings about a total reversal, it is impossible to break this psychological construct of a Hindu. It is this clean-unclean distinction that reflects the hierarchical power relations in the cultural plane, in both the dominant and the subjective states. Those who dominate and those who are dominated are in a system that has multiple factors: on the basis of the colour of skin, the house you live in, the street, the town, the work place, place of worship, the language you speak, the food you eat, dress, the articles you use signify both the relationship between them. Though basically this relation is about possession or lack of wealth, at the cultural level, and at micro levels, beginning with man-woman, superior-inferior, parent-child, father-son, mentor-disciple, this hierarchy is formed at the subconscious level. It is established in its full significance as dichotomies: as haves and have-nots, ruler and ruled, capitalist and worker, and capital and labour. In short, class status is achieved and caste status is ascribed. They are not interchangeable.

The Merits of a Place

The hierarchical order referred to above has been described in detail in *Periyapuranam*. Since there was no compulsion when it was written to be discreet and hide these differences among people, the book talks freely and openly about them. When Sekkizhar explains the qualities of a place, the hierarchical order is revealed. Before the age of the epics, while describing the good qualities of a place, the tradition was to portray the productive mountains, forest, fields and seashore. After the rise of Brahminism in the Tamil country, the situation changed and in *Periyapuranam* the merits of a place is expressed only in terms of the varnashrama dharma prevailing in that place. While describing Kodungolore, the birthplace of a Nayanmar named Kazharittarivaar, Sekkizhar says that the greatness of a place is proved by the manner in which the four-fold caste order, the dharma of the Vedas, is followed implicitly there. In an inscription at Karandhatankudi, near Thanjavur, attributed to the Chola king Kulothunga II, there is a reference to a place where 'the caste order, justice and ethics are followed'.[7] The words 'the people inferior to the brahmins' in the inscription found in Karandhai leave no doubt as to who presided over this caste order.[8] Not only Sekkizhar, but the brahmin saint Sambandar, whom he praised in poems, has also written hymns along similar lines. While glorifying a place Sambandar, unfailingly talks about the priestly acts of the brahmins living there, and how they recite the four Vedas and conducted ceremonial fire.

Periyapuranam brings out the difference between the habitations of brahmins and those of the inferior castes prevalent during the times of Sekkizhar. He praises the town of Sirkali, the place of Sambandar of Kauniya Gotra, which was surrounded by paddy fields and where the harvest was plentiful. There was a big temple for Siva, he goes on to add, the priests conducted yagnas, and there were patasalas where brahmin boys memorized the Sama Veda. In Seynjalore, the birthplace of Visarasarman, a Kasiba gotra brahmin, there

were patasalas and yagna salas. Sacred cows moved around
the streets. Brahmin boys were carrying the material needed
for the fire ceremony. Brahmin girls were returning from
their baths. Priests were hurrying in chariots after conducting
yagnas. Next comes a description of Saththamangai, the birth
place of Neelanakkan the brahmin. Here brahmin priests
raised three types of sacred fires: *aagaavaniyam, kaarugapa-
thiyam and Thakkanaakini.* Alongside, as the fourth variety of
fire, virtuous women raised the fire of Chastity.

While Sekkizhar admires the birthplaces of brahmin
devotees as having admirable brahminical features, he does
not have a good word for the places from which devotees
like Kannappan and Nandan originated, as they came from
hunter (Pulaya) castes. Kannappan is from Udupur of Kalathi
hills. Here the Kuravas, like Siva, hunt wild animals in the hills
where the hunting tribe lives like criminals. They rustle
cattle. There is no love or fear among these dark-skinned
people. By birth they are criminal-minded. Brahmins live a
life of luxury in an area of fertile paddy fields. Nandan lives
outside a village called Aadhanur, in a clutch of huts among
the fields. The Pulayas are dark skinned. They rear poultry
and dogs, and plough the fields. They play the parai and
drink toddy. Pulaya women pound paddy and sing. They
decorate their tresses with paddy panicles, drink toddy and
dance. Sekkizhar terms such dwellings of the Pulayas as
'the habitations of the lowly'. He does not even find it fit to
name the village. Traditionally, even today, the habitation
of the dalits is outside the village. Even the houses built for
the dalits by the government are usually outside the town in
places labelled 'colonies'.

In one place you have the sacred fire, sacrificial pit,
ceremonial bath, chanting, the cow and similar 'clean' things
while in the other place you have the slaughter of animals,
thievery, physical labour, dark skin, toddy, dogs and such
'filthy' features of the hierarchical order. It can be observed
that one place has prosperity and is a centre of sanctity while
the other, on the margins, is without these features. From

the manner in which Sekkizhar describes a place it is clear that in his view this is the nature of things.

The town of Chidambaram has been idealized as the pinnacle of purity where three thousand brahmin priests lived. Sekkizhar praises these brahmins as 'divine vedics who need no more privileges'; they have mastered the four Vedas and the six limbs (angas) of the Vedas (*Siksha, Chanda, Niruktha, Jothisha, Vyakarna and Kalpa*).[9] They are engaged in six kinds of occupations that have no connection with real socio-economic production and they are incomparable. These priests wielded immense power during Sekkizhar's time and a few centuries earlier. All other Saivite devotees considered themselves subordinate to them. The place where these three thousand priests gathered was known as 'the Big Assembly' (*Perambalam*). They gathered there, heard cases and dispensed justice (see *Nilakanta Puranam*). For a dalit devotee like Nandanar the very thought of approaching this assembly was frightening. The Siva temple at Chidambaram was the centre of priestly power. Sekkizhar asserts that the North Indian brahmin priests and South Indian vellala landlords are the reason that 'the vedic culture flourished, and Saivism shone'. Brahmins are identified as the source of the vedic culture and the vellala landlords as the protectors of Saivism. One should not forget that the vellalas gained immense cultural authority by nurturing brahmins in the Tamil country. Today, when the method of agricultural production has changed and technical, scientific and bureaucratic systems have intervened, the basic economic dominance has changed. We have to observe that only after the brahmins became dominant in this new dispensation did the laments of the vellalas begin.

Forms of Devotion

In *Periyapuranam*, not just in the place, but even in the forms of piety towards Siva expressed by the devotees, there is a gradation of higher and lower, according to each one's caste and occupation. It has been emphasized that though piety can be expressed in whatever manner one wished, still such expression should not violate caste rules. While permitting an individual to have beliefs and worship practices according to his/her conscience, the vedic brahmin leadership was keen that the rules governing each individual should not be ignored. This situation still continues. But today, in addition to the six traditional functions, brahmins have taken up jobs which they eschewed earlier as polluted (particularly in dealing with cadavers to learn Western medicinal practices, and in the leather industry producing shoes and chappals). On the one hand, brahmins decry caste-based reservation for government jobs, on the other hand, they have gone to court and got a judgment that only a brahmin can officiate as a priest in a temple. It is common knowledge that a brahmin gets his powerful position by officiating in priestly obligations/positions.

The brahmins among the Saivite Nayanmars were all priests and that was their way of being devout. Sambandar, a very learned young man, is projected as travelling around Siva temples, singing hymns. According to mythology, immediately after his wedding in his sixteenth year—and even before the nuptials—we learn that he merged with Siva. Among all the devotees of Siva, he has performed the largest number of miracles. He has resurrected the dead and healed deadly diseases. He destroyed his arch enemies, the Jains, and is said to have converted a king to Saivism. Appar, another Nayanmar, also did similar acts. (Converting kings to Saivism is usually a fable.)

Periyapuranam talks about certain Saivite devotees, who have not written any hymns, such as Visarasaruman, Neelanakkan and Naminandhi, who have demonstrated their devotion by working as priests according to their caste tradition. Seven-year-old Visarasaruman, who had gone through the sacred thread ceremony, watches the seniors anoint a linga with milk and he too conducts the same ceremony. Under the fig tree on the banks of a river, he makes a linga of sand, collects milk from the village cows and anoints it, like the young girls who play the game of 'homemaking'.[10] This is just an amusement for him. The story makes the point that a child of a brahmin household will follow the calling of the caste. Neelanakkan also spends the day worshipping Siva. So does Naminandhi who lights the lamps in the Siva temple daily. A Chola king makes him a priest in a temple. The king sets up endowments in the temple to provide food for the devotees as part of the daily rituals.

There is no reference to any vellala caste devotees, who were next to the brahmins, as serving priests. Their piety was expressed through their agrarian practices and philanthropic activities. Appar is the important figure among the vellala Saivites. He is also known by other names such as Marulneeki, Dharumasenan, Navukarasan and Vaageesan and wrote a number of hymns.[11] So, the profession of his caste is not mentioned. Still, it is said that he cleared the surroundings of the temple of grass and so we can surmise that it was agriculture-related work. He in fact did the job of weeding which is related to cultivation.

The other vellala devotees followed worship codes according to their tradition of agriculture and philanthropy. A vellala Saivite believer by the name of Arivattan donates cooked rice, spinach, and mango pickles to a Siva temple. Another vellala Saivite votary named Kotpuli gives a superior variety of paddy to a temple so that the devotees can be fed. Another farmer, Kundaiyur Kizhan, gives sacks full of paddy to Sambandar. Many rich vellalas built Saivite monasteries and fed brahmins and others, each separately. It had been laid down that it is the duty of the vellalas to provide food from the produce of their caste occupation, agriculture, to ascetics, hermits, guests (new to the house) and devotees. Another Saivite literary work *Thiruvilaiyadal Puranam*, written around the seventeenth century, describes these vellalas as 'opulent farmers', and 'those who make donations and grants'. It says that the vellalas wait for guests to visit, seat them close to themselves and feed them. They appreciate literary works and reward the poets. They ably support the king as ministers.[12] The Sathaga literary works also gives a similar account of the vellalas. The inscriptions from the tenth, eleventh and twelfth centuries confirm this situation.

Next in order, the trading communities also follow a pietistic regimen according to their caste vocation. The countryside and villages surrounded by paddy fields were the centres of vellala dominance. In cities like Poompuhar and Pazhaiyarai in the Chola land, traders under the name Nagarathar were the dominant force. The traders mentioned in *Periyapuranam* are all city dwellers. The sea-faring traders lived in cities along the coast. Born in Karaikal and married in Nagapatinam, Punithavathi, from a trading caste, is projected as one who goes by the rubric of being a woman rather than a Saivite devotee. Her husband discards her as 'one with Divine power' (in other words, educated). She eventually ends up as a singer for dance recitals in a Siva Temple. In fact she seeks this position and gets it. In those times women expressed their piety only by sweeping the temple, applying cow dung paste on the floor, stringing flowers, drawing kolam and by singing and dancing during festivals. Punithavathi sang and Thilakavathi, another female devotee, swept and cleaned the floor of temples.

The caste occupation of a trader from Pazhaiyarai named Amarneethi was selling cloth. He expressed his devotion by providing free underclothing to Saivite devotees. Murthy was a trader in sandalwood and he donated sandalpaste daily to the Siva temple. Next comes the artisan caste. The devotees of this caste group also showed their piety according to their caste tradition. Neelakantan, a Saivite from the potter caste, makes begging bowls of clay for some devotees. Another Saivite from the barber caste, Siruthondar, was trained in warfare and became a commander in the Pallava army so he did not have to do priestly duties. However he fed devotees

and fulfilled his religious obligations. A Saivite follower from
the caste of oil-pressers, named Kalian, showed his piety
by supplying oil for the eternal lamps in the Siva temple.
Kanampullan harvested grass as fodder for the cattle, sold
it and out of the proceeds provided oil for the lamps in the
temple. Nesan, a weaver, made clothes for Saivite believers.
Enadhinathan, an Ezhava, trained men in swordsmanship
and with the money earned, helped some devotees.

Neelakanta Yazhpanan is from the Panar (musician) caste
which is placed lower than that of artisans. He, along with
his wife, strums his yazh and sings at the temple entrance.
A man referred to as Thirukuripu Thondan (his real name
is not given) from the washermen caste, washes the clothes
of devotees gratis. A tribal hunter Kannappan offers Siva
the meat of the boar he hunted. Nandan from the Pulaya
caste ekes out a livelihood by making agricultural implements out of cowhide. He supplies hide for drums and other
percussion instruments and strings for the veena and yazh
and also ingredients for puja. That is the way he shows his
piety. Sekkizhar makes it clear that from the high priests
of the Chidambaram temple to the lowliest Pulaya from the
slums, votaries of Saivism from all castes demonstrated their
devotion to Siva according to the tradition of their caste.
But all these demonstrations were done with the temple as
the fulcrum.

Space

Earlier, in the section on the qualities of a place, we observed
that space is divided according to gradations of caste. Now we
can see a different kind of hierarchy related to space. We can
discern this particularly in the lives of brahmin and vellala
saints like Sambandar and Appar. It is common practice
to make a gradation according to age. Appar might have
been seventy and Sambandar just sixteen. So according to
Indian tradition, Appar is a senior and Sambandar being

junior should respect the former. This does not happen in *Periyapuranam*. It is Appar who is willing to prostrate at the feet of Sambandar. This seniority according to age is valid only within the same caste, but between brahmin and vellala castes it does not hold good. Being a brahmin, the boy becomes superior to the elderly vellala man. Appar is one of the palanquin-bearers for Sambandar. Appar's head and Sambandar's feet become equal. When Sambandar calls Appar, the latter answers, 'Here I am, your servant'. Similarly, all the wealth of a trader named Amarneethi is not equal to the underwear of a brahmin. Only when he and his wife stepped onto the scales of the balance along with their properties, did they become equal to the underwear. A Panar, a musician by caste, could not compose music to a complex and intricate hymn written by Sambandar. Complexity and intricacy are projected as the caste skills of a brahmin.

Carnatic music and Bharthanatyam also took shape in this manner. Among the non-brahmins the gradation within each caste may be valid. But it is emphasized here that when compared with the brahmins this hierarchy is not acceptable. What is considered 'lower' among higher castes is emphasized as higher among the lower castes.

Processions

The scenes of processions described by Sekkizhar indicate the extent of dominance in space. The receptions extended by vast crowds of people in the towns of Sirkazhi, Tiruvarur and Vanji to illustrious devotees such as the Perumal, Chera king, Sambandar, Appar, and Sundarar, are depicted in scenes of procession.

Sambandar gets the power of writing hymns even in his third year after he drank milk from the breasts of goddess Parvathi! Observing this miracle, the brahmins of Sirkazhi and other Saivite devotees celebrate. They decorate the principal street with plantains and areca nuts and carry a sacred vessel (khumbam) in the market street. Along with a host of priests, a vast concourse of devotees joins in and they throw their upper garments in the air, and shout 'Hail the holiness of Veda! Hail the vedic disposition'. Women join the festivities and throw puffed rice, flowers and perfumes and welcome Sambandar. A similar reception is given to Sundarar who persuaded a crocodile to regurgitate the infant it had swallowed. When he visits the town of Vanji in Chera country, he is given a royal welcome. Women perform dance forms like sadhir and kunalai koothu in the streets. Brahmins chant the Vedas. Appar, who miraculously escaped the wrath of the Pallava king, also receives a joyous welcome. During the festivities, celestial beings like the devas, kinnaras and others shower flowers on him and blow horns.

In those days epics and ula (procession) literature talk about kings participating in pageants in the main streets after a victory in battle. The latter day tanippatal poems refer to political party conferences, religious pageants, temple car festivals and Ganesha festival processions, all reflecting the power play of the leaders. In the military parades conducted by the government this dimension is demonstrated clearly. By going in procession in the main streets of the town, the right of dominance is established symbolically. Through the sound of exultations and of musical instruments, the authority of the hegemonic caste is forced into the ears, dinned into the eardrums. Wherever you see the king's face or wherever he looks, that demonstrates his power over that place. Women on whom he sets his eyes are delighted that they are within his sphere of authority.

Events like pageants invariably move the masses emotionally wild. Their social roles and obligations are temporarily disrupted. It is as if they are all in a trance. The mask of normality is shed. They sing and dance. They discard their upper garments. In *Periyapuranam*, brahmins and others momentarily relax their rigid caste positions and mingle. Women closeted in their cubicles come out and sing. They sprinkle

flowers on those going in procession. After this brief reversion of the usual order, they go back to their original positions
in the hierarchy. It is evident that these pageants and marches
were the venues of expression of reversions during the Bakthi
movement. Such events increased manifold in the form of
pageants conducted for kings, and later, festivals for gods
and temple chariot ceremonies. In the desire of people to
have the procession of gods come through their streets, one
can see an aspiration to share power. The procession of
gods established the dominance of the upper castes. Not just
icons of gods, but even their symbols were taken in procession in the streets of the upper castes. In the present day,
when the procession of one religion goes through the streets
of people of another faith, voices of objection are raised
because the procession is seen as an assertion of authority.[13]

Miracles

Now let us look at the 'miracles' performed by Siva for Saivite
leaders and his devotees in return for their demonstration
of piety (slavery) towards him. These have to be examined
because even Siva's miracles have been performed bearing
the caste position of each benefactor in mind. When the
three-year-old brahmin infant Sambandar cries, to satisfy his
hunger, Parvathi expresses her breast milk in a golden cup
and feeds the child. Immediately after being fed, the child
begins to sing his famous hymn 'The One Who Sports an
Earring' (*thodudaiya seviyan...*).

The child Sambandar is given a palanquin adorned with
pearls and an umbrella similarly embellished so that he need
not walk and strain his feet. As if these were not enough,
Siva *ganas* (demons) invisible to the eyes of people, spread
a canopy of pearl umbrellas over the palanquin to guard
him from the heat of the sun. Though no one in our times
believes in these miracles what has to be noted in this account
is that Siva goes to great lengths to take care of a brahmin

toddler. Similarly he is generous with gold, food and women when Sundarar asks for these. When a brahmin child in play anoints a linga, Siva admires him, accepts him as his own son and embraces him. He makes him the leader of his followers and confers on him a high position, as Chandeesan. He is given the privilege of wearing and displaying Siva's weapons, jewellery and costume. The fabrication that the twice-born brahmins close to Siva will make it straight to heaven to be with Siva when they die is revealed in these accounts.

Next to them, we see how different is the dispensation of Siva's bounties to landlords and kings. When the brahmin Sundarar and Chera king Perumal journey to Mount Kailayam (Kailash) to see Siva, Perumal rides a horse while Sundarar rides Siva's gift, a white elephant that flies through the air. Siva who organized a comfortable journey for Sundarar, accepts him but refuses to admit Appar, a vellala, and Punithavathi, from a trading caste, to Kailaylam however much their bodies have been deformed in penance. Old man Appar walks all the way to Kailayam. He rolls across mountains, his shudhra body utterly destroyed, and reaches Siva in the form of a soul. But the Lord refuses to show himself and asks the devotee to go to Tiruvaiyaru where he promises to appear. Likewise, Punithavathi, who gives up her body as a 'source of sin' and reaches Kailayam by 'moving on her head' because she considers it disrespectful to walk on foot towards Siva. 'My daughter', says Siva and according to her wish asks her to go to Tiruvalangadu temple where she is authorized to sing for his cosmic dance. As a woman she does not even ask for a place in Kailayam.

Siva himself does the chores for brahmin devotees, ignoring the two from vellala and trading castes. He bestows boons only on these two after they nearly shatter their (shudra) bodies. When we forget God for a moment and examine the scene, we observe that it is Brahminism which created the gradation of upper and lower as the basis of the scheme of things. Vedic Hinduism is a religion that gives prime place to

the brahmin. This can be observed even today. For brahmins
and other upper castes close to them, if there is no brahmin
officiating, then household ceremonies and temple worship
are unacceptable, and all the ceremonies appear to violate
what the Sastras have laid down.

One can discern the 'partiality' of Siva by observing the
varied ways in which he bestows benefits on Sambandar and
Appar. To open the doors of a temple that had been closed
for a long time, Siva persuades Appar to sing ten hymns. But
to close the doors of that temple he makes Sambandar sing
just one hymn. (Appar's hymns were of great literary merit
and so Siva makes him sing ten songs.) The twentieth-century
vellalas have an explanation for this: because Sambandar's
song was very ordinary, he was given a chance to sing only
one. This justification may be acceptable from the point of
view of an anti-brahmin stand but we have a different view
on this.

It takes time to open doors that have been closed for
long. Once opened, it does not require a lot of time to close
them again. But all such explanations are given to cover the
favouritism of Siva in dealing with these two devotees. It looks
as if Siva was fair and that the brahmin was a scoundrel. Siva,
who sports a sacred-thread, was not an ancestor worshipped
by the hunting tribal society of yore. One has to bear in mind
that he has emerged as a vedic god, with a partiality to sacred
fire and vedic chants. To blame the brahmins and at the
same time accept their brahminic ideology is nothing but a
hegemonic tendency to make oneself a brahmin. So what is
emphasized here is that one hymn by a brahmin is equivalent
to ten hymns by a vellala. A brahmin is that much superior.
Next we see when Sambandar and Appar enter a temple, Siva
first appears in front of Sambandar. Then Sambandar draws
Appar's attention to this appearance.

There are more such events. During a severe famine, Siva
gives some gold coins to Sambandar and Appar to feed their
followers. While giving the coins, he keeps the lot meant for

Sambandar in the eastern altar and the coins for Appar in the western altar. What is significant here is that the eastern altar is in front of the sanctum and the other is behind the sanctum. Sambandar will receive grace from the front while Appar will get divine favour from behind the sanctum. This confirms the order that favour from the front is superior to favour from behind. Moreover, the coins given to Sambandan are easily exchangeable but Appar's are not!

Divine Interventions

Other than those mentioned above, the divine favour that Siva dispensed to devotees such as those from vellala, trader, artisan and untouchable castes was different. To begin with, framed according to caste status through severe tests, Siva checks whether their devotion is genuine, and only then does he proceed to grant favours. Even this business of granting favours is not very transparent. If we consider them as divine interventions, then even in that activity we can see a gradation. When Siva intervenes in the lives of his devotees, he takes care not to violate the caste order in any way. To help his followers Siva takes many human forms: an old priest, a brahmin bachelor, a licentious Saivite brahmin, a Saivite yogi and an ascetic North Indian. Then he appears in dreams or as a disembodied voice. Lastly when he is taking them along with him, he appears sitting on his mount, a bull, along with his consort. Here the form of an old brahmin priest is assumed only to help Sambandar, Sundarar, and, as an exception, Appar. Siva conducts Sundarar's marriage with a girl from the Saivite courtesan caste. When Sundarar gets thirsty and hungry, Siva sets up a shed and with lime rice and water awaits his arrival. It has to be noted here that according to the Manu code a brahmin can accept food only from another brahmin and that rule is adhered to here. If he accepts food from someone lower in the caste order, then the receiver gets polluted. So to prevent Sundarar becoming polluted Siva takes the form of a brahmin. *Periyapuranam* explains this concept even more explicitly in another context. One day lunch has not been sent to Sundarar. Siva, who cannot bear to see Sundarar hungry, takes the form of an old brahmin priest. He goes about with a silver bowl, seeking alms in brahmin households and feeds Sundarar. It would be pollution if he collected food from non-brahmin houses. It can be seen that Siva strictly follows the brahminic code of cleanliness. Uncooked food like paddy, pulses and vegetables can be accepted by brahmins from non-brahmins. It has been laid down that such food articles are not polluting. *Periyapuranam* says that according to this code, Sundarar accepts the cartfuls of paddy and pulses that Kundaiyur vellala sends. Maybe the pollution vanishes in the heat of cooking! That is true. To remove pollution from the Pulaiya body of Nandan, he was asked to pass through fire. But castes like vellalas can eat the food cooked by brahmins. There is no pollution there. To establish that in such cases there is no ritual pollution, *Periyapuranam* narrates an instance in which Siva takes the form of an old brahmin and offers lime rice and water to a starving Appar.

Let us now look at the case of Sundarar. Siva, who gave him food and quenched his thirst, also takes care of his sexual needs. At Tiruvotriyur he gets a girl (who has been living in the temple) married to Sundarar as a second wife. *Periyapuranam* refers to some vellalas and traders giving their daughters to temples and to brahmins like Sundarar. Sastras have laid down that brahmins, who are prevented from eating food cooked by non-brahmins as it is polluted, can however accept women from other castes.

Sundarar's first wife, learning about his second wife, chases him out of the house when he returns. Good show! To sort out Sundarar's problems, Siva assumes the guise of an old brahmin priest and goes to mediate with the first wife. Since she refuses any compromise, he assumes his original form as Siva, and manages to unite them. Apparently the

Lord will go to any length to help a brahmin disciple. The interventions Siva made in the lives of other devotees are different. Particularly in the case of the weaver caste, the oil presser caste, the toddy tapper, the vedar (hunter) and the Pulaya caste devotees, some traders and vellala believers, there persists a belief, that only if they take their own lives, deform a limb or kill their children or wife, will Siva intervene. Then too his interference will only be through a disembodied voice or a dream. These interventions reflect the economic and class conflicts of the period. The 'high-caste' people who have exclusive right to own land and a share to the income from it, attain the comforts and luxuries of worldly life without any physical distress or labour. The other castes that eke out a livelihood by being artisans and cultivators, however much they toil, at times are deprived of even basic food to sustain themselves. This world and the nether world are comfortable and cosy only for the brahmins and vellalas. For the rest, death comes as liberation.

III

Inversions

Inversion means turning upside down the basic and agreed upon human identities ethics, social mores, and traditional/ hereditary aspects which are revealed in the cultural plane. To retain forever a particular mode of production, the gradation operating between the production forces is based on conflict and violence. The struggling productive relations (such as exploited and the exploiters) in the cultural plane, space, home, food dress, habits, ethics, rules, and language have all been turned into symbols without challenging these cultural symbols and codes, unchanging at the subconscious level, constructed by language, one cannot oppose the hegemony of exploiters at the economy level. So, in order to bring revolutionary changes in the productive mode in the casteist Indian social set-up, we have to invert the dominating and dominated meanings that operate in each person's sub-conscious mind, that is, those ideologues and symbols which are expressed by us in unconscious ways as 'pure', have to be inverted. These kinds of protests are understood by domi-nant forces as rebellion. But for the dominated people, this kind of inversion is a kind of subaltern warfare! Just as the people get used to the dominated condition, they should also get used to struggling through inversion. In the Indian context, to rouse the fighting spirit of the people oppressed on the basis of caste for millennia, it is essential to have viola-tions and inversions on the cultural plane.

You may ask what is the connection between this kind of inversion and the type of inversion mentioned in *Periyapuranam*? During the Saivite pietistic wave, for a given period, temporarily at least, morality and justice as accepted by the society were ignored. Lower-caste people and women, due to devotional ecstasy, breached the code of conduct laid down for each stratum. These transgressions are referred to as 'reversion'. Let us look at some of the explanations for such transgressions.

Reversions of Morality and Justice

Before the Bakthi movement, Jain and Buddhist faiths that preached renunciation and control of the senses gave rise to a number of ethical works in the Tamil country. Keeping these works as models, the vedic Hindus also produced ethical works. Murder, robbery, drinking and brothel visits were referred to as heinous crimes. Chastity (karpu) was held to be an exclusive virtue for women and considered divine. Respecting elders, honouring one's father, a wife looking upon her husband as a god, men not coveting others' wives but considering them as deities, caring for those who seek help and the things that are entrusted to them safe custody, men liberating themselves from sexual cravings, entertaining guests, engagement with the task undertaken . . . and so many other moral codes were laid down.

In the incident described above another idea is revealed. The conflict between Visarasarman and his father reminds one of the Vaishnava puranic story of the Prahalad *vs* Hiranyan clash. Sekkizhar has incorporated similar episodes not only from other sects but from folklore, mythology and folk beliefs into the stories of Saivite devotees narrated in *Periyapuranam*. Like the son who kills his father in pietistic ecstasy, in *Siruthondar Puranam* which is part of *Periyapuranam*, there is a story about a father and mother slaughtering their son and cooking the flesh.

Siruthondar, born in the Maruththuvar caste, had taken a vow to feed Saivite believers. To check if he would keep the vow and provide the food sought by the devotee, the kind and compassionate Siva takes the form of a wandering hermit. He goes to Siruthondar and tells him that he would like to eat his infant son. With alacrity, Siruthondar and his wife together kill their son, place the head aside, cook the rest of the body and serve it. The hermit wants to eat the head also. The couple cook the head. The hermit persuades the couple also to eat.

When you see such merciless brutalities one after the other it is evident that this is ritualistic imagination. God asking for the first born, single male child, is not uncommon in other religions. In the Old Testament, you have the story of the bearded old man God, seeking the sacrifice of his devotee Abraham's only son. In patriarchal society this is one of the myths built around the first born male, next only to the father.

In real life, at least in one sect of Saivism, a similar practice has been in vogue. Human sacrifice of the first born male has been recorded. Similarly, from inscriptions we learn of a ritual called *Navakandam* in which a devotee slits his own throat in the presence of a crowd, either for the victory of a king or for any other such supplication. *Periyapuranam*

records two such incidences of the *navakandam* ritual:
Kaliyan, a worshipper from the Chekkar (oil presser) caste
donates oil to keep the lamps burning in the village temple.
When he has trouble getting oil, he tries to sell his wife and
buy oil. Since no one would buy his wife, Kalyan slits his
throat and gives blood in place of oil. Likewise, Arivataayan,
a devotee, brings rice, greens and mangoes in a basket. He
trips, falls and everything tumbles out of the basket on the
ground. Considering it a desecration, in a rage he slashes his
own throat with a sickle.[14]

From Siruthondar onwards we read about a number of
Saivites maiming themselves or those of someone close to
them. These are all inversions of justice. What is to be noted
here is that all those whose limbs are maimed violently are
non-brahmins. Kalikamban of a trading caste severs the hands
of his wife for having delayed giving water to a devotee to
wash his hands. A wealthy vellala man, Kotpuli, kills his whole
family including his parents, wife, siblings, relatives and slaves
who used up the paddy stored for Saivite devotees during
famine days. He goes to the extent of killing an infant that was
breast-fed by a mother who partook of that rice. A believer by
the name of Eyarpahai kills the people who try to prevent his
giving away his own wife as alms to a brahmin. Kanampullan
uses his long tresses of hair to keep the lamps burning in a
temple. When sandalwood paste is not available, a merchant
by the name of Murthy rubs his elbow and offers his bone
marrow for ritual use. A Pallava king, Kazharchingan, cuts off
the nose of his wife's because she smelt the flowers meant
to be offered to Siva in worship. He also cuts off the hand
with which she picked up the flowers. Ekalibakthan knocks
his head against a stone. Nandan walks into fire; Kannappan
gouges out his own eyes.

Jain and Buddhist ethical works condemned such doings
as murderous, sinful acts. But *Periyapuranam* extols these
self-destructive acts as expressions of pietistic ecstasy. It has
been projected that Siva himself commends these acts. Even
if the devotees of Siva violate normal conduct, the codes of

this world, on another plane Siva neutralizes these acts by granting heavenly status to those who were victims of these violations and to those who committed the violations. The acts of breaching normal codes are hailed as superior acts as per the protocol of 'the world above', from a ritualistic point of view. Such presentations are not only seen in works like *Periyapuranam*. During the crusades that took place in the West, and the Islamic jihads also, such unjust hegemonic acts were carried out in support of superior notions.

Only lower-caste people have been depicted as people who express their piety by torturing themselves, injuring their bodies. Even these violations are related to different castes in the hierarchical order. It must be noted here that Brahminism projects each caste as having its own characteristics from birth. Brahmins are like cows. They are peaceful and non-violent; the kshatriyas are less non-violent but are regal. The vaishyas are less regal, and have a certain degree of peaceful nature but a lot of inferior characteristics. The shudras have very little royal character, and a lot of inferior quality. All this has been described in the Bhagavath Geetha which says that each caste has its character that is inherited through birth.[15] Here it must be noted that in addition to saying that brahmins are pure and non-violent and that the others have mixed characteristics in various degrees, another feature is pointed out. The peaceful nature attributed to a brahmin is completely absent in a shudra and in fact he is the very opposite of a brahmin; his qualities are negative, tamasic (dark and degraded). If you observe the inversions described in *Periyapuranam*, they have been placed in a one-above-the other order, according to varnashram dharma laid down in *Manusmiriti* (the code of Manu).

Caste and Pollution Inversions

One of the basic features of the Bakthi movement is the participation of many castes. The agrarian life was spreading, and the folk cultural features of the tribal people from the

mountains who came in waves to join this society played a
part in it. Their female-mother deity worship too, all this gave
the necessary impetus to the Bakthi movement. The tribal
people given to exogamous marriage practices were slowly
absorbed into the caste structure of the brahmins who were
and are strictly endogamous. The brahminic hegemony was
used to bring the tribal people into the caste structure. The
brahminic-vellala combine was keen that these new entrants
to the caste structure were relegated to the lower order in
the formation. However, from among these new entrants,
artisans and warriors got Sanskritized by the passage of time
and managed to gain a higher place in the caste hierarchy.
Inscriptions tell us that after the twelfth century a number of
artisan castes grew in status by granting donations to temples.
Some other castes have been recorded in epigraphs tracing
their origin to the sacrificial fire pits raised by brahmin rishis.
Gradually, under different pretexts, Brahminism absorbed
the features of the lower castes' folk culture. Different trends
were laid down in these castes and among them a gradation
was established. The Female-Mother deity worship of these
people was modified and accepted as Shakti worship. This
work was cleverly executed by Adi Sankarar (eighth century).
In male dominant Saivite temples, a separate shrine for the
Devi was established and female worship was accommodated.

In the brahminic view the practices of these lower-caste
people were seen as polluting and unclean. To the brahmins
the culture of these people appeared tainted. To tolerate these
features, during the Bakthi movement they devised stories of
interventions by Siva, voices and dreams, to meet the situation.
Such instances have been described in *Periyapuranam*. Even
during the Bakthi movement you could hear voices of protest
against caste. Such opposition could not be avoided. But this
dissent was Sanskritized and neutralized by Brahminism.
We learn from *Periyapuranam* how a small priestly clique can
perpetuate its hegemonic hold, eschewing weapons, using
only clever tricks.

For instance, in Sathanur a man called Moolan, of the shepherd caste, became a student of a siddhar called Sivayogi and eventually he himself became a siddhar. He grew so learned that he could write a book titled *Thirumandhiram*, with anti-caste overtones. But *Periyapuranam* has projected this in a different way. Bitten by a snake, Moolan lies dead and Sivayogi, the siddhar from the Himalayas enters the corpse using his powers of transmigration. By attributing the anti-caste voice as coming from Siva, Brahminism reduces it to a ritual and defuses it. When any one of the brahmins who are born to be learned, or the vellalas, wrote hymns, brahmins commended them as the work of a child of God. When a cowherd grew philosophical through contact with a siddhar and wrote a treatise, the credit was not given to him but to one who had lessons from Nandi Deva, the mount of Siva, in other words to one connected with hegemonic power.

In *Periyapuranam*, women and lower-caste devotees are portrayed as pollutants. Through acts of piety these people breach rules of ritual practice and purity. To accommodate these violations Brahminism uses the interventions of Siva at a ritual level. For the upper caste to face the disruption caused whenever rules of purity are infringed dreams and disembodied voices are used as a device. In other words, dreams and voices appear as a connection between hegemony and violations. We have to note that when these two realities are in conflict with each other, the hegemonic side uses that conflict to suit its convenience by adopting dreams/voices at a ritualistic level and thus solving the problem. Whenever there is any protest or a threat from the suppressed, the hegemonic people will adopt clever conceptual devices to divert their attention or defuse the disagreement. This is true even in the present technological-scientific age and it was true during the agricultural period of yore. There are other views about the dreams of suppressed people. But this essay is not the place to discuss them. The dreams and voices presented in *Periyapuranam* are the reversions of an oppressed

people. They are regularized through Siva and these reversions are used to project them as provisional rituals. One can
even say that Brahminism has followed this device throughout history. Truth to say, we have to view these as momentary
ritualistic safety valves brought in to avoid such reversions
in real life.

Let us now take a look at such reversions and compromises.
From a hygienic point of view it is correct to view all that
is excreted from the human body as dirty. But Brahminism
extends this idea further and mystifies those excretions as
'pollutants'. This pollution concept has been formed in such
a way that in day-to-day life it suppresses, in an ideological
manner, the working-class people and women. Saliva from
the mouth is considered a pollutant. In *Periyapuranam*, the
wife of Neelanakkan, a brahmin priest, tries to blow a ven-
omous spider away from an idol of Siva and some droplets
fall on the icon. Though these could have been wiped away,
to the brahmin who is fixated with pollution, this appears
an unbearable violation. The spittle of a woman falling on
the icon seems to be the height of contamination. In a rage,
Neelanakkan abandons his wife and returns home. To adapt
this transgression suitably as an 'episode' to a brahmin priest,
the very personification of hegemony, Siva appears that
night in his dream and instructs him to go and look at the
idol in the morning. When the priest goes and sees he finds
that except in the place where the droplets of his wife's saliva
fell, the other parts of the statue show ulcers caused by the
sting of the spider. He reconciles with his wife. Thus a ritual
is performed here. In a spirit of ecstasy, the transgression is
miraculously accommodated.

Likewise, when devotees from the lower rungs of the
caste structure behave in ways beyond their caste status, Siva
appears in their dreams, and transforms these violations
into rituals. Neelakanta Yaazhpanan and his wife are from
the untouchable caste of Panar. According to custom they
stand outside the temple, play on the yazh (harp) and sing

in praise of Siva. According to caste tradition they are denied entry into the temple. If they entered the temple it would be a violation. What *Periyapuranam* says is that such an entry can only be an act of God and not a human act. Accordingly, Siva appears in the dream of his devotees and says that he wants the 'Panars' to enter the temple, sit in front of the sanctum and sing. This miracle takes place due to divine intervention. A transgression of a caste rule is accepted and presented as a marvel. We have to bear in mind that even if God intervenes, he intervenes by supporting Brahminism. The same 'Panar' couple sing as usual at the entrance of the temple at Tiruvarur. Though by divine grace they were able to go up to the sanctum and sing in the Madurai temple, here in Tiruvarur they could not enter the temple! The reason is that what happened in Madurai was not on the plane of reality. Otherwise a similar development should have taken place in Tiruvarur. Siva had to intervene here also. For the Panar couple to enter the temple, a special way is created. It was nothing but a brahmin ploy that created a new entrance instead of taking them through the path meant for all devotees. A separate entrance, special status, singular honour, divinity for women, all these are done not with the aim of honouring that person but with the opposite effect. It announces an act of noblesse oblige. The act of honouring someone itself proclaims the superior-hegemonic status of the one performing that act. Similarly even today, there are separate crematoria and paths leading to them for lower castes such as washermen, 'Ezhavas' and 'Kammalar' and we know what kind of honour operates here. This is one of the many dimensions of untouchability. Even reservation for jobs and college seats can be looked at from this angle.

The way Lord Natarajan at Chidambaram appeared to the Pulaya Nandan is also quite similar. Nandan, who is scared even to enter the periphery of Chidambaram, turns in the direction of the temple town and worships the earth. Night and day he circumambulates the compound wall of the temple. An untouchable entering the boundary of the town, the power centre of brahmins, would be a transgression none could even dream of. Again here through Siva, a ritual is performed. Siva appears in the dream of a dikshithar (high priest) and instructs him to raise a sacred fire, let Nandan be consumed in the fire and then send him to Siva in the form of a brahmin sporting a sacred thread. This is also intimated to Nandan through a dream. The priests gather at the southern entrance (direction of the God of death) and there in a pit they start a fire. They ask Nandan to get into it. He circumambulates the pit, gets into it and comes out alive. Now they do not see the Pulaya Nandan. Instead a hermit with matted hair and sacred thread is seen. As is customary, kinnaras, celestial beings, shower flowers and play musical instruments. Nandan enters the town sporting a sacred thread. He goes up to the edge of the Dance Hall of Natarajar and then disappears mysteriously. A complex ritual is over. Though Siva made him go through this rigmarole, the Pulaya Nandan till the end did not enter the sanctum. Nor did Siva appear to him, as he did to the other devotees, on his bull mount, along with his consort.

We can see the transgression of Nandan from another angle. Pulaya Nandan's body being consumed by fire is not as atonement for his sins. His very birth as a Pulaya is considered a sin here. For such a sin, he has to be consumed by a fire lit by a brahmin. We can compare the punishment given to Nandan to the one meted out to a brahmin who committed an offence in *Thiruvilaiyadal Puranam* in an episode concerning a heinous crime. A brahmin youth has sex with his mother and slays his father and Siva appears before him in the guise of a lowly hunter and suggests the following as penance:

> He should eat only once a day, that too by begging for food.
> He should get up before dawn, gather grass for the cows and feed them.

Should do errands for Saivite devotees.
Should bathe in the temple pond thrice daily.
Should circumambulate Siva108 times.

Tiruvilaiyadal Puranam says that if he does these penances for three months, 'he can assume the form of a divine brahmin who has repented'. As a punishment for his misconduct, a brahmin is asked to beg, to eat only once a day, or to do errands and to cut grass. In day-to-day life, the bulk of the working class, do these chores daily for a living. The upper-caste brahmin as atonement for the offences committed by him has to do what the people of low caste do in their normal life. What is emphasized here is that the normal life of the lower castes is in fact a punishment for their very birth. *Periyapuranam* says that to shake off the sin of being born low-caste, the Pulaya body has to go through a sacred fire started by a brahmin.

Only the body of Nandan is noticed here. Only if this Pulaya body is destroyed will there be salvation says the *Puranam*. Other than the brahmin devotees, some vellala believers and some Kammala untouchable devotees have been presented as sinful, polluted bodies according to their caste ranking. According to their sinful forms, the bodies are maimed, burnt, stabbed, or chopped up. *Periyapuranam* says that it is only after this that they get salvation or get to view the gods.

Brahmin devotees Sambandar and Sundarar reach Siva without a scratch. Note that others do not get this privilege. In particular a woman can stand before Siva only as a skeleton. What is pointed out here is that it is only a brahmin male body that is the ideal of purity. Even when Siva assumes the form of a human, he carefully does so only in a brahmin body to appear before brahmins and a few vellalas. Later as devotees come from lower rungs of the caste structure, Siva takes the form of a yogin, a hermit and an impure brahmin. Eventually to a believer who is a washerman he appears as a beggar. For the untouchables, who are below all these categories, Siva never appears. He speaks to them as an astral voice or appears in a dream. In *Thiruvilayadal Puranam*, the mother of a brahmin who commits a misdeed is made into a hunter woman. Siva appears in the form of a kuravan (a bird trapper) to that sinful brahmin. What Brahminism says here is that a brahmin who commits an act of moral turpitude deserves to be in the body of a low caste. All this is a result of looking at the body and its labour as ignoble. Manual labour is polluting!

Let us look at more instances of reversion on the caste plane that occur in *Periyapuranam*. Naminandhi, a brahmin priest, mingles with other caste people in a festival and thinks he is polluted. He asks his wife to give him some water to clean himself. Siva appears in his dream and explains that all those people in the festival are in fact his army of Siva *ganas* (mythical dwarfs). The next day Naminandhi goes to Tiruvarur where the event took place, checks the facts and is convinced.[16]

When a brahmin loses purity Siva appears in a vision or in a dream and explains away the ignomy. But with a trader by name Eyarpagai, Siva acts differently. This trader treats all the devotees of Siva equally irrespective of their caste. Siva is not impressed with Eyarpagai's egalitarian outlook. He assumes the form of an impure brahmin and asks Eyarpagai to give him his wife. It was a practice among trading and agricultural castes to offer their women to brahmins as gifts. We learn through *Periyapuranam* that a merchant gave his daughter Poompavai to Sambandar and a farmer gave his two daughters as largesse to Sundarar. But in this instance a brahmin asks a merchant devotee to gift his wife to him. In a cultural tradition which has many moralistic voices condemning coveting another man's spouse, a brahmin seeks the wife of someone lower in caste status. Another important point has to be noted here. By asking for the wife of someone who treats everyone equally, ignoring the caste protocol, the caste standard of the merchants may be lowered. This is because Brahminism believes that the purity of a caste depends on the genital activity of the women of that caste. We have to note that in this instance it is not just caste pollution, but female sexuality that is also connected.[17] When the brahmin asks for his wife, Eyarpagai informs his wife quite happily. Though initially hesitant, she agrees to the proposition and gets another crown as the one who views her husband as a god.

But the relatives of Eyarpagai are furious over the development. They are up in arms considering this an affront and a disgrace to their caste. However Eyarpagai holds piety far superior to caste honour and kills all the relatives who oppose him. Many caste wars originate from a concern for caste purity and to conserve the endogamous marriage system. In particular, the functioning of female sexuality forms the basis for the purity of each caste. Men may tolerate anything but not a woman of their caste having sexual relations with a man of another caste, particularly a man from a lower caste.

We have to examine why Siva is out to create such a blood-bath in this case. Here the power of patriarchy is ritually legitimized. While caste cleanliness is emphasized, another fact is also projected. With the brahmin community Siva does not take such liberties. He does not organize any test to check the purity of that community. In this story he does that only for the merchant caste. What is to be inferred from this is that Brahminism encompasses within its ideology not only caste hegemony but also patriarchy.

Let us now take a look at the story of Kannappan, the hunter, and learn about another dimension of the Bakthi movement. According to the tradition of his people, Kannappan follows the practice of folk deity worship. He offers broiled wild boar meat to Siva; this kind of worship is not according to the vedic worship done by priests. Sivakesari, the brahmin priest who offers flowers and water to the gods, finds this offering of meat and bones nauseating. He goes into a rage and shouts, 'This is pollution. Who did this?' And then as usual to accommodate this ritually, Siva appears in the brahmin's dream and

declares that he considers the saliva of Kannappan holier than
the water of the river Ganga and that the boar meat offered
by the hunter is tastier than the food cooked in the sacred
fire by the brahmin. (In the pantheon of gods, Siva was originally a hunter who later began sporting a sacred thread. Maybe
because of this primordial memory, Siva is shown to prefer
boar meat in this story.)

Here, Siva temporarily violates the ranking of 'upper and
lower status' for Ganga and the saliva of the hunter, brahmin's
food and hunter's boar meat. As pointed out earlier it is
not common in real life: It is a temporary ritual. This ritual
reinforces the real beliefs. All the instances of transgressions
of normal rituals are used to fortify at a subconscious level the
day-to-day practices. In fact only if we practise these rituals of
binary opposition in our daily lives, is there respect for the
rituals and the exaggerated emotional expressions that they
cause. This is the reason behind the ecstatic entreaty of a few
Vaishnavite saints to be a stepping stone of a temple and a
fish in the temple pond. One can observe such gradations in
Christian and Islamic devotional literature also and in the
teachings of their preachers.[18]

Appar says that he will bow to one:

> Even if he is a beef-eating Pulaya
> If he is a devotee of Siva who bears
> the Ganga on his matted locks.

Nammazhwar writes:

> Even if they are the lowest of the four-fold of castes,
> Even if they are the lowly of lowliest,
> If they are Krishna's devotees then he would be their slave.

Vipranarayana writes:

> Even if they kill the many life forms,
> And burn and bury them,

If they are given to contemplating Vishnu,
They will not have to pay for their crimes.

All of the above three instances are examples of ritualistic, ecstatic states of inversion and not real experience. Words such as 'even' betray the real nature of the statements. Moreover, in literary tradition, they are manipulating poetic license. It is like saying 'Even if the sun rises in the West'. The story of Kannappan and Nandan are dramas that teach us the above lesson.

Through the episode of Kannappan we also learn something else. We see that the brahminic religion has by its tricky devices assimilated the practices of folk deity worship prevalent among tribal, semi-tribal and lower-caste people, along with their dance, songs, animal sacrifices, street drama and trance. There is more. The description of Sambandar curing snake bite and dangerously high and persistent fever through chanting of mantras is also in the realm of folklore. Using chants to heal comes from the tribal tradition. In the Bakthi movement, devotees dancing in groups, going into trances and jumping around, singing, rolling on the floor and throwing clothes in the air are all features of folk deity worship of tribals.

I must point out another related feature. The brahmin-vellala leadership which had assimilated elements from the worship practices of different castes had appropriated many stories from other religions and had incorporated them in the episodes relating to the saints. It has been pointed out earlier that the story of Chandeswara echoes the legend of the Narasimha avatar. In the Karaikal Ammaiyar episode, the outline of the Jain tale from the epic *Silapathikaram* can be seen. In that epic and in the Karaikal Ammaiyar story, husbands from the merchant community (Chettiar) leave their wives and live with other women and each begets a daughter. There is similarity even in naming these infants. In the Karaikal Ammaiyar story, the newborn girl is given the

name Punithavathi, which is the name of the first wife. In
Silapathikaram the mistress declares that the girl is the child
of the first wife Kannagi. After losing her husband, Kannagi
became a goddess whereas the wife Punithavathi becomes
a ghost and a singer of devotional songs in Aalangattu
temple. Both stories originate in coastal towns in the Chola
country, Nagapatinam and Poompuhar, and reach their final
denouement in the Pandya country. In the course of time
as the Bakthi movement which absorbed many traditions,
legends and cultural features grew, so too did land-owning
authority and brahminic sacred powers, becoming an all-
powerful vedic hegemonic structure. It is this development
that *Periyapuranam* documents.

The two kinds of transgressions we have seen were symbolic of the social change brought about by the early Bakthi
movement. Later in the grip of the brahmin-vellala hegemonic structure they gradually morphed into ritualistic
signs and devices of the poetic tradition. This is clearly indi-
cated by *Periyapuranam*. It is claimed that Sekkizhar wrote
Periyapuranam in such a way that it drips with piety. We saw
in our analysis so far what is dripping from that work. There
is sufficient evidence in inscriptions, as in *Periyapuranam*, to
establish that in tightening their hold on society by nursing
the caste structure, the vellalas were as culpable as the brahmins of those days. If the caste edifice crumbled, they stood
to lose. If the caste system continued it was misery for the
artisan castes, for the untouchables and for those who toiled
on farms. To try to move up in caste ranking was no solution either. That would mean accepting the brahmin-vellala
leadership. It would also mean increasingly brahminizing
one's caste. So the answer is to abolish the caste system. For
this, first, the Hindu religion will have to be modernized.
Inter-caste marriage, inter-dining and exogamous marriages
are the means to this goal. The hegemonic signs that have
been imprinted in our subconscious minds and in our attitudes have to be eradicated through some 'ritual'. Rebellion

should be a natural process. Eventually, through confrontation with a society that is not structured around caste or religion, without caste, without religion, the brahminic-vellala power structure will be destroyed. That is inevitable. Let us wait and see.

Most of the Saivite saints about whom Sekkizhar gathered material, as mentioned earlier, belong from the sixth to the ninth centuries, in other words, the Pallava and Pandya periods of South Indian history. These Pallavas were not of Tamil stock.[19] They were a powerful tribe from southern parts of India and were responsible for certain new movements in the Tamil country. There are some inscriptions that refer to them as 'those who cleared forests'. They cleared the jungle in the Thondaimandalam area and extended agricultural tracts.[20] During this period, some of the tribes and semi-tribes in the mountainous area and highlands also began to develop agricultural practices. In the process many of them were absorbed into the Hindu caste-religious system. The Pallava royal families called themselves kshatriyas and in turn they patronized the brahmins. The king was brahminized, meaning that he was accepted by the brahmins. He needed the temples, Saivite and Vaishnavite, along with the priests and sacred fires to legitimize his sovereignty over the people and the land. Fertile and productive paddy fields were donated to the brahmins who facilitated this process through the rituals in which they officiated.

It was during the Pallava days that Saivism took the Tamil country by storm. It was an emotional movement. A high degree of ecstasy and frenzy was evident. Song and dance were dominant. The elation and celebrations were not part of the original brahminic way of worship. These features were from tribal worship rituals and from the veneration of the female deities of the rural subalterns. These developments have to be seen along with the advent of the Pallavas and the involvement of tribal people in agriculture. It is the passion of these tribal people that formed the basis of the Bakthi movement. Its momentum transcended caste barriers. The Sanskritic-brahminical concept of pollution was discarded, as discussed earlier, through the story of the hunter Kannappan, narrated in *Periyapuranam*. The Bakthi movement was resilient and generous. Utilizing this force, the agricultural clans and landlords brought the urban traders under their control. It was this interaction that was behind the struggle between Saivism which was vedic and Jainism which was non-vedic. But later, after the tenth century, during the period of the imperial Chola kings who was completely brahminized, the Bakthi movement petered out and social formations rigidified. Finally the society, firmed up by brahminic ideology, took the form of Hindu casteist society. The power over people went into the hands of vellala-brahmin leaders. It was at this period that *Periyapuranam* appeared.

From those days till today, in Hindu society, whenever forces from the marginal areas, the landed areas and the hill areas meet, there is turmoil followed by disintegration, destruction and the appearance of a new hierarchical order. This dynamic has been repeating itself over time. When the wave of the Bakthi movement that affected the Tamil country spread to the northern part of India during the eleventh century thanks to the work of Vaishnavite saint Ramanujar, it created similar undercurrents. In Sikhism, also, one can observe the hierarchical caste system. In Karnataka, the Lingayats secured a high position in the order. Caste rigidity in Hindu society loosened slightly. In the much later freedom struggle of the twentieth century because of the emotional involvement of people, after the advent of 'our own' rule, caste-religious formations rigidified to control the new centres of power.

What is to be understood from these developments? In Hindu society change is permitted only within the given structure. Brahmins and those upper castes who managed to gain hegemony over the working-class castes will never tolerate any alteration in this structure. Max Weber, to reiterate, had said that 'before everything else, without caste there is no Hindu'.[21] This is not only a historical truth but for a Hindu it is also a personal, distinct and psychological reality. *Periyapuranam* talks about these truths without any attempt at hiding them.[22] The author of this work, Sekkizhar, accepted Brahminism fully, in the Saiva vellalas age of the *Periyapuranam.*

We apply this to the Saivites who joined the anti-brahmin movement at the turn of the twentieth century. During that period, vedic religion that had been nurtured by the Bakthi movement was suitable for an agricultural society. The land-lords of that society, Udayars, landowning castes, imposed their hegemony on the lower-caste people toiling in the fields. The social structure based on the brahminic caste edifice was designed appropriately to make the landlords feel that they were entitled to the service of this working class. It was advantageous for the brahmins as well as the landowning vellalas to make the working class believe that in this birth, it was only through physical labour that one could work out one's karma. This helped to keeping them eternally at the base of the social, economic and political structure as low castes. For providing them with this device for exploitation, the vellala landlords gave the brahmin priests vast tracts of wetland, as we have seen earlier. In return the priests attributed vedic origins to the vellala castes. The hegemonic signs that have been imprinted in our subconscious minds and in our attitudes have to be eradicated. Rebellion should be a natural process. Eventually, through confrontation with a society that is not structured around caste or religion, without caste, without religion, the brahminic-vellala power structure will then be destroyed. Let us wait and see.

Notes

1 For the socio-political background that has been briefly touched on here see Burton Stein, *Peasant State and Society in Medieval South India* (New Delhi: Oxford University Press, 1985).

2 Some historians refer to the Pallavas as tribes that were progressing. They were not kshatriyas. They are compared to the Chandragupta Maurya dynasty which established the Magadha kingdom in the North during 600–500 BC. The Pallavas, after they became kings, were baptized as 'kshatriyas' with the blessings of brahmins.

3 In Thondaimandalam (present day Vellore, Trivannamalai, Cuddalore districts) Vanniyars are said to be connected with Pallava tribal people on the basis of their clearing of forests by felling trees for agriculture. (Thus the collective memory of cutting trees to extend agricultural land in those times now manifests itself among the Vanniyars as 'Road Blocking' agitation.)

4 'Before everything else, without caste there is no Hindu', Max Weber in Thomas C. Ertman *Max Weber and Indian Religions* (New York: Cambridge University Press, 2017); electronic book.

5 Earlier, K. Kailasapathi in his Tamil article 'Pulaipadiyum Gopurava-salaum', and N.Vanamamalai in an article in his journal *Araichi* criticized *Periyapuranam* from a sociological angle. Ma. Po. Sivagnanam wrote a rebuttal to Kailasapathi.

6 Richard Lannoy, *The Speaking Tree: A Study of Indian Culture and Society* (New Delhi: Oxford University Press, 1974): 214.

7 Dr. A. Kritinan, *Kalvettil Vazhviyal* (Chennai: Manivasakar Pathippagam. 1991):125.

8 Ibid. p.123

9 The six limbs are chanting, teaching, raising sacred fire, teaching fire rituals (yagna), philanthropy, and accepting donations. The first four refer to reciting Sanskrit Vedas in temples and in other rituals. Accepting donations refers to receiving gifts from kings, landlords and nobles. They have to live through the things they get from chanting and fire rituals. Some of the gifts these people get are cows, gold, young women, cultivable land. Philanthropy is a quality of kings and vellalas rather than of brahmins.

10 In *Thevaram* hymns and in Sekkizhar's descriptions, after listening to the chanting of brahmins, parrots also chant. Similarly watching the devotees worship, monkeys imitate them.

11 Bearing many names is a sign of power. God was given a thousand names. Though Siva is one God, he is known by different names in each of the Siva temples in Tamil Nadu. Some landlords of the Chola country had the titles of the Chola emperor as a prefix to their respective names. Kings also assumed many titular names such as

Arikesari, Rajakewsari, Tiribuvana Chakravarthi, Gangaikondan, and Kataramkondan. The town of Seerkazhi, the birthplace of Sambandar, was known by twelve different names and he had written some anthems using these diverse names. However, you do not come across this multiname feature with the lower caste-devotees. In fact we know only their nicknames such as Eyarpagai, Kanampullan, Tirunalaipovar and Kannappan.

12 Paranjothi Munivar, *Thiruvilaiyadal Puranam*, '*Tirunagara sirappu*', songs 54–55.

13 Ranajit Guha, *Elementary Aspects of Peasant Insurgency in Colonial India* (New Delhi: Oxford University Press, 1983). This is about the Munda rebellion in the eighteenth century against the East India Company and against local bandits. Also see Guha and Gayatri Spivak, eds, *Selected Subaltern Studies* (New Delhi: Oxford University Press, 1988).

14 Like the instances of slitting one's throat described in *Periyapuranam*, the book also talks about cutting off the tongues of those who malign Siva or his devotees. A believer by name Saththi, gets hold of some people who defame some Saivite devotees, pulls their tongues with tongs called *thandayam* and slices them with a knife. He is hailed as one who carried out an act of piety. Maiming various parts of the body as a punishment was in vogue in those days. *Manusmiriti* describes instances of cutting the ears and tongues of shudras for having listened to the Vedas. Punishments like disfiguring the nose and chopping off the hand were also common, particularly for women.

15 Srimath Bhagavath Geetha (Tiriuparaithurai: Sri Ramakrishna Tapovanam, 1974): 4th Chapter,13th sloka.

16 In *Thriuvilayadal Puranam*, a brahmin learns by overhearing a conversation between some messengers of death (Yama's messenger) that when a woman was due to die according to her fate, an arrow caught among the branches of a tree, came down and killed her. But he is convinced of this rule only when he sees a cow butting and killing a bridegroom in a wedding house because his time was up. He has to see another death to be convinced of the rule. In Brahminism there is a sadistic strain towards the suffering and agony of others. They live comfortably through the hard work of others; yet the bodies of that working class are considered polluted and the people as born out of sin.

17 One should approach *Periyapuranam* from the angle of gradation of people, of reversions and from a feminist angle also. We have to check how this book looks through the angle of patriarchy, at Karaikal Ammaiyar, Thilakavathy, Mangaiyarkarasi and other women characters. We should pay particular attention to instances of selling women, gifting them, sharing as sex objects, donating them, marginalizing them, maiming nose and hands.

18 In the New Testament of the Bible there is a parable of a poor widow
    who offers two copper coins. God prefers that to the offering from the
    rich and wealthy. This is also recounted as an ecstatic statement and
    not real.

19 See n2.

20 Vanniyars are said to be connected with Pallava tribal people.

21 See n4.

22 See n5.

4

Brahmins, Vellalas and the Tamil Country

I

People who have lived for thousands of years in a socio-economic political structure held together by religion, land, the joint family system and a self-sufficient economy, have had to face drastic transformations. The revolutions that took place in eighteenth-century Europe stood their lives on their heads in the last two hundreds of years. For the first time in Europe, cities, trading capitalist class, middle class, factory workers, voyages to exotic countries, patriotism and multiple communication facilities came into being. In order to plunder the raw material needed to meet the demands of the new methods of production, to sell surplus products and earn profits and to find new lands (markets) Europeans undertook long and arduous voyages. The stories of the ancient wealth of eastern lands brought by the sailors motivated European merchants to capture new markets for their products. The new hegemonic scheme was really to create capital rather than to annex lands.

The European trading companies that landed in the eastern and western coasts of the Indian subcontinent understood the oppressive and obsolete methods of the Hindu and Muslim kings. They found an archaic society that functioned on the basis of caste decided by birth and religious fanaticism.

When the Dutch, the French and finally the British came to the southernmost portion of the Indian subcontinent, they found the Telugu- and Tamil-speaking brahmins, vellalas and some kshatriyas functioning as the dominant powers.

II

The Europeans recognized that the brahmins were at the helm of Hinduism and the graded caste structure while the vellalas had a hold on the politics and the economy. Even during the time of the Pallavas, brahmins were accepted as having acquired divine authority (see Essay 3). Later, on the basis of the Puranas, mythology, Smrithis and Dharmasastras, the brahmins made the Pallava kings and other kshatriya kings accept the form of puranic Hinduism that was formed when the varied tribal forms of worship were homogenized. This happened from 200 BC onwards long before the vellala Cholas of Tamil Nadu metamorphosed into kshatriyas in AD ninth century. The Chola king Rajasooyam Vetta Perunarkilli and the Pandya Palyahasalai Muthukudumi Peruvazhuthi are old examples of this kind. Through literary works of the Pandya country such as *Paripadal* and *Kalithogai* we can learn about the spread of puranic Hinduism in the southern Pandya country and the brahmins who spearheaded it. From the days of the early Cholas, who ruled before the Pallavas, the brahmins functioned as the ideological leaders of the Pallavas, the later Cholas, the Pandyas and the Nayak rulers. There are a number of inscriptions about the 'Brahmadeya villages' which were given to the brahmins as gifts by the vellala, kshatriya kings.

The kings of the period ensured comfortable financial status for the brahmins who were at the helm of puranic Hinduism. In return the brahmins endowed the rulers through the principles of Sanathana dharma, temples, the gods, rituals, and customs with the power to rule. In the process the brahmins safeguarded their own hegemonic position. Later, when the Chola reign gave place to Pandya rule, ridden with infighting, Malik Kafur who came from the North to plunder, and then the sultans who ruled Madurai for a while, looted the Hindu temples in the custody of brahmins, according to Ibn Batuta.[1] To prevent this, to guard brahmins, Hindu temples, Hindu religion and themselves, the Telugu Nayaks captured the Tamil country and for nearly three hundred years imposed Sanathanic torment on every village.

Earlier, the brahmins pleased the 'shudra' landlords, Pallava, Chalukya, Rashtrakuta, Maratha, Bana kshatriyas who, in return for their chanting the Vedas and fulfilling other ritual needs, had given them fertile lands. During the Nayak rule, the brahmins supported the Andhra Aaraveedu, Sangama, Chaluva, Thuluva Nayakas. After the arrival of Europeans on the scene, the brahmins who shunned the local dalits as untouchables who ate beef, now got closer to the white men ignoring their beef-eating. First, they acted like middlemen. Later, the children of the brahmins left the Brahmadeya villages, went to cities, acquired degrees through English education and reached good positions in government and social circles.

III

In the hegemonic order, next to the brahmin-kshatriyas were the landowners and politically powerful vellalas, and below them the artisans, agricultural castes and below them, the working class, which was subjected to many pollutions projected by the Hindu rites and rituals, came the bulk of the Tamil people. During the beginning of the later Chola period (800–1300), the vellalas with titles such as 'Velaan', 'Araiyan', 'Udayaan', 'Aazhvan', 'Kizhavan' were the dominant forces on non-Brahmadeya villages. It was they who exercised matters related to land rights and royal obligations that had been delegated to them. When the later Chola rule ended, these people became powerful landlords.[2]

When the Andhras began ruling the Tamil country from the fifteenth century onwards, the Andhra rulers and the Telugu high-caste people who supported them got access to landholding that was dominated by the vellalas and also to the administration of the villages. During this period the practice of leasing the vast stretches of land given as grants to temples and gods came into being. If you look at the situation in those days, kings, Saivite-Vaishnite temples, and the Saivite and Vaishnavite vellalas (Tamil and Andhra) who had hereditary landownership (kaani) were the landowners. The vellala joint familes collected what was due to the kings and also extracted their own share of the produce.

During the Vijayanagar empire, when the Andhra vassals ruled the Tamil country, the pattern of village administration changed to the Andhra model. New posts sprang up in the administrative structure. In the Tamil village administrations, official posts such as Senabovar, Gowda or Reddy, Thalari from Andhra, morphed into Karnam, Maniam, and Thalaiyari. For the upkeep of the officers and men of the Andhra and Kannada forces, lands were granted under the category of 'Padaipparru'. New Nayakkamangalam villages sprang up. To supply armies to the Telugu kingdom, Palayams were formed in Tamil Nadu. They were also called Palayapattu.[3]

The villages given as grants during the Andhra rule were of three kinds. Those that came under the Andhra ruler were 'Pandaravada'; those allotted to the Poligars and the Amaranayakkars were called 'Amara' villages; and the third category of villages meant for miscellaneaous religious chores were granted to the brahmins and referred to as 'Maaniyapoo'. The Maravar commandants of Pudukottai, Sivagangai and Ramanathapuram, along with landlords and the descendents of the old Pandya dynasty who ruled from Tenkasi, compromised with the Andhra rulers and continued their rule.

When the European 'company' traders arrived in the Tamil country, built forts in harbour towns and started their commercial activity in Cuddalore, Tharangambadi and Chennapatinam, the dominant groups in the Tamil country were the brahmins, vellalas and a minority group of kshatriyas. The kings and landlords from Andhra were also included in the group. After about three hundred years in the Tamil region some of the Andhra vellalas and brahmins had mastered the language and could write poetry in Tamil.[4]

As discussed earlier, the vellalas were connected with land-ownership, royal and religious chores. Slightly lower-caste Hindus were the artisans and those who were not connected to occupations related to power. Below them were the farm-hands, cattle minders, sanitation workers who were the untouchables. From the days of the Pallavas, temples, royalty and those authorized by the royalty had the right to own slaves. It was the practice to have documents drawn as 'Till the Moon lasts, I and my descendants will be hereditary slaves'.

IV

The identities of caste, family and authority that are pre-dominantly determined at birth, the ideology of patriarchal society, were prevalent for centuries in the Tamil country. Only after the arrival of Europeans, the ideology of the Western bourgeoisie, governmental structures and the ideas of the European Renaissance were systematically introduced into the Tamil region. Along with Christianity, came many new things: monthly salaried jobs, the educational system created for that purpose, the three-tiered teaching methods, the English language, textbooks, the printing presses that produced them, publishing houses, property-ownership laws that could not be modified easily, the rules of the judicial system, the police and the prisons that protected it, com-munication facilities like railways, post and telegraphs, and magazines. In the social and political changes brought on by the above interventions, the grumbling of the salaried class, the voice of the native entrepreneurs, the competition among the traditionally powerful castes to get a foothold in the newly emerged power centres and their place in the political scene began to manifest themselves.

Let us now examine how the traditional dominant powers of the Tamil country, brahmins, Saivite-Vaishnavite vellalas, confronted these new changes. Before the arrival of the Europeans, during the rule of some non-Tamil dynasties, these two caste groups did not have to face the different cultural structures relating to the Hindu religion, caste rituals, and patriarchal societal values. Though Tamilians accepted Muslim rule which introduced a different religious culture, their rule was spasmodic intrusion and did not create a lasting impact. The Andhras, who were outsiders, migrated in large numbers when they were ruling the Tamil country. They followed the same caste hierarchy that they adhered to while in Andhra. In the Tamil country too they followed the same gradation from Aaraveedu kings to the cobbler caste. When British rule was established in the Tamil country with the gun and the Bible, along with it came Western culture which was in conflict with Hindu religious and caste traditions. This created mixed consequences among the brahmins and the vellalas.

For the brahmin who wielded the sanctified authority of Hindu religion, the spread of Western culture created an ambiguous situation. The mores of the beef-eating white man, with his utter indifference to caste and rituals initially came as a shock to the brahmins. At the same time, to participate in and enjoy the benefits of the new politico-economic order they had brought about, the brahmins were pushed into a situation in which they had to accept the values of the white man. The brahmins, who have been recognized as the authorities in the Vedas, found the secular content in the English education, which was the path to power, a trifle disconcerting.

During the seventeenth and eighteenth centuries, a small group of brahmins, along with vellalas, acted as agents for

European traders to collect produces from the interior. But in the nineteenth century this changed drastically. Realizing that their tricks could no longer work, brahmins began to move out of the Brahmadeva villages which they had received three hundred years ago as gifts from shudra rulers. They moved to Chennai and other cities, to gain English education and attain positions in the power structures of the government. Though they left their traditional authority behind in the villages, after they acquired degrees and got jobs like assistant collector, tahsildar, munsif, the authority they could exercise doubled. Along with the old Sanathanic leadership, brahmins now assumed new positions of power.

To suit the new economic production structure, the people of the old landowning society were recast by the European capitalist-liberal ideology. The British rulers realized that unless the Indian casteist, religious orthodoxy was broken, they could not muster the forces for their new modes of production. Hindu orthodoxy had already began to thaw through the new system of education, the judicial system, jurisprudence around the individual, government job opportunities, laws raising the minimum marriage age for women, conversion to Christianity and the spread of urban culture. For the low- and middle-level caste people who had no other choice than to accept the profession determined at birth by caste, new job opportunities opened the path to higher social status. Observing this change, brahmins began to bring in modifications in the rubrics of orthodoxy. Children from traditional brahmin families did not hesitate to enter medical education which called for dissection of cadavers and work with skins and hides in the godowns of Bangalore. As private property increased, there was demand for the service of lawyers. Laws centring on the individual, the breakdown of the joint family, members from one family taking up diverse jobs, with varied income, strict documentation of rural landownership, legal transfer of properties, police stations and law courts—all these developments led to opportunities for degree holders to become lawyers and judges and earn handsomely. Many of these lawyers would later enter Swadeshi politics. Nearly 90 percent of the lawyers in the Tamil country were brahmins.

In the new landscape, brahmins could not mix easily. They could not easily give up the archaic, rural joint family system, vedic leadership, the rituals and ceremonies that differentiated them as twice-born from the other castes. For the educated brahmin this hesitation to enter the new order acted a subjective obstacle. To exercise his traditional authority, the brahmin needed orthodoxy (*aacharam*); similarly to use the new authority they had to make some compromises. They nursed aacharam inside their homes but outside, in offices, in colleges, in law courts, conferences, reformist associations, in magazines, and in fiction they fulminated against the canons of orthodoxy. Thus they presented themselves as pioneering representatives of modern ideas. The brahmins, who had wielded only religious authority so far, acquired enormous direct political and economic power during European rule.

V

Meanwhile, the position of the vellalas in the Tamil country was different. Working as merchants and rural landowners, the vellalas enjoyed the benefits from paddy fields, hymns like *Thevaram* and *Thiruvasagam*, erotic poems of the bards, the company of courtesans, temple trusteeship and gourmet food, along with electuaries, sweetened medicines, for digestion. They lorded over the lower castes and the untouchable farmhands. When their dominance ended and the British took over the control, the aristocratic vellalas realized that the brahmins had already seized a great part of the authority generated by governmental power. Without having to unsheathe their swords they learnt the way to become new 'poligars'. Some of these vellalas became Christians and attained high posts in the British government.

In varied ways the vellalas confronted the new situations created by British rule. Some vellalas, led by people like Yazhpanam Nallur Arumugam Pillai *aka* Arumuga Navalar, opposed the Western missionaries and the Christianity they propagated while accepting British rule. He thought that his duty was to guard his Lord Muruga and Saivism against attacks from Christianity. He was particularly keen to save the caste honour of vellalas who stood for the Saivite tradition. He could not tolerate the violations of caste rules by the English-educated caste Hindus and brahmins. He bitterly attacked Ramalinga Adigalar, a nineteenth-century saint, who preached a liberal, Saivite path free of caste, called 'The Path of Equality' (*samarasa suddha sanmargam*). He went to the extent of calling his wife a woman of ill-repute. He accused Ramalinga Adigalar of a lack of grammatical knowledge and went to court against his poetical work *Thiruarutpa*.

The following passage establishes that he was a Saivite Sanathani who supported British rule.

> Some of our Saivite friends, for the sake of food, clothes, books and education allow their children to eat in the house of padres along with children of lower caste and in the process violate the codes of their caste and religion. Yet they do not hesitate to be proud of themselves as Saivites and as people of high caste. Shame, shame (*Pirabandhathirattu:* 53–54).

His whole purpose was to prop up the cause of Saivism and the vellala caste. Some of the Saivite monasteries in Tamil Nadu supported him in this campaign. People like Arumuga Navalar can be described as the residue of an orthodox tradition that is disappearing.

The main element in the vellala reaction was raising its protest against the brahmins. We might call it vellala politics. There were three trends: led by Maraimalai Adigal, Justice Party leaders and E. V. Ramasami Periyar.

Maraimalai Adigal eschewed political struggle and was comfortable with British rule and English education. To combat the brahmins on the socio-cultural plane he wielded Saivism and the concept of Pure Tamil as ideological weapons. He spoke on topics such as 'The Vellala Civilization', 'Saivism Is nothing but Ancient Tamil Canon', and 'The Religion of the Tamils in Tamil Nadu and in Sri Lanka'. The idea that the religion of the yellalas was Saivism and that the civilization of the Tamils was vellala civilization was spread by him. In Tamil Nadu and in Jaffna organizations like Saiva sabhas, Saivasiddhantha mahasamajams, Saivasiddhantha sabhas and Saivaprakasa sabhas came into being and grew active. The patrons of these outfits and those who lectured in them were all vellalas.

The work of bonding Saivism, Tamil and vellalas went on briskly. Saivite saints of yore like Manikavasagar, Thirunavu-karasar became the symbol of vellala pride. Saivite monas-teries, Karandhai Thamizh Sangam, The Thamizhsangam of Pandithurai Thevar, the magazine *Senthamizhselvi*, the pub-lication outfit Saiva Siddhantha Noorpathipu Kazhagam were all active in nurturing the tradition of vellala Tamil scholarship and Saivism. The second, was the rise of the bourgeoisie in Tamil Nadu as a result of the British impe-rialism in which the brahmins were in the majority. But in the larger social structure the people who acknowledged the vellalas as the leading caste formed the greater part.

To ensure political gain out of this preponderance and to capture power, the new concept of 'Dravidians' came in handy for the Tamil vellalas, and the Telugu and Malayali upper castes. Identities such as Tamil, Tamilian, vellala and Saivite were relegated and Dravidian and non-brahmin identities were projected. The rajas of Bobbili and Panagal, Raos, Rajulus, Telugu Chettis, Malayali Nairs, vellalas of Tamil Nadu along with some educated Adi Dravidas formed the South Indian Liberal Foundation also known as the Justice Party. In the diarchy established by the British (1919), only those who owned property had franchise, and the Congress, whose appeal transcended caste and religious boundaries, had boycotted the elections. Against this background, the Justice Party won the elections. During the periods 1920–21, 1923–26, 1930–32 and 1932–37 only the Andhra Dravidians were premiers in the Madras Presidency.

Let us look at the third factor, the Self-Respect movement of Periyar which was an anti-brahmin movement. After 1927, under the leadership of the Kannada vellala Periyar, also known as E. V. Ramasami Naicker, the concepts of Tamil-Saivism were ignored and the ideology of Atheism-Dravidam was taken forward. Periyar believed that the basis of brahminic authority was puranic Hinduism and that only if this was demolished, could brahminic hegemony be dismantled. It was emphasized that atheism should be taken up as an ideological weapon if the brahminic race were to be brought down and if the Dravidian race had to redeem its self-esteem. Even though in principle caste and religious dominance was not acceptable in the new bourgeois structure, in the social set up the Tamil country due to the varnashrama canon of Hinduism, temple ceremonies, family rituals connected with marriage and death, brahmins held a prime place in the scheme of things. The Self-Respect movement opposed this primacy. The new generation of educated vellalas and the people below them in the caste order and the backward castes were active in this movement.

VI

Before I conclude this essay, let us look at the connection between Tamil and vellalas and what was gained by Tamils by the vellala movement. From the beginning of the his-torical period, brahmins were involved in the chanting of Vedas, rituals and the study of Sanskrit. They could persuade some kings to follow Sanskritic culture. We observe that most of the kings who ruled in various parts of the Tamil

country during the Pallava and Chola times had accepted
Sanskritic culture. While this was the situation in the upper
stratum, it could be seen that the majority of the people
had absorbed the culture of indigenous people along with
the tenets of Sanskritic culture that was spread through the
Hindu temples.

When we look at Tamil scholarship, literature, we notice
that except Sambandar, Sundarar and some Azhwars, the
bulk of the poets and devotees were all non-brahmins,
particularly vellalas. Sengundha Mudaliars claim to be the
descendants of poet Ottakoothan while some vellalas claim
descent from Kamban, author of the Tamil *Ramayanam*.
The teacher–pupil lineage that lasted till the beginning of the
twentieth century were vellala lineages such as Pillai, Chetti
and Mudaliar Kanchipuram Mahavidwan Sabapathi Mudaliar,
Mahavidwan Meenakshi Sundaram Pillai, Somasundaram
Pillai, Muthuveera Upadhiyayar, Koozhaithambiran, Neer
Veli Sankara Pandithar were all well-known vellala scholar-
teachers. For about two hundred to three hundred years
these vellala scholars have been writing about the Saivite gods
and their dalliance with bosomy female deities. They earned
some money by describing the processions of zamindars, commandants and vellala philanthropists and how the women
who watched them were so aroused that the sandalwood paste
on their breasts dried and crackled with the heat of desire
and how the breast-band snapped. The Tamil language they
had nursed was converted into one of the instruments to
fight the brahmins in the twentieth century. It turned out
to be a revivalist work by the vellala movement and it spoke
about the glories of ancient Tamil. The educated brahmins
engaged strongly with the efforts at creating a new literature.
We will look at this later.[5]

Professor P. Sundaram Pillai of the vellala movement
studied the lives of Saivite saints. Vedhachalam Pillai
(Maraimalai Adigal) researched Manikkavasagar. They wrote
in English about the past glory of Tamils. To meet the need

for textbooks that arose when the system of English education was introduced, the upper castes published epics, Puranas, Saivite hymns and grammar contained in the palm leaf manuscripts.[6] What started as a textbook publication greatly facilitated Tamil revivalism, publishing the palm leaf manuscripts that lay neglected in Saivite monasteries and in the homes of vellala scholars brought them both fame and wealth. New publishing outfits were established. The old palm leaf manuscripts became saleable commodities in the new market of education. The publishing houses and book stores were owned by the traditional merchants, the Chettiars.

Vellala Dravidian politics received an impetus with the printing of a two thousand-year-old anthology of poems, *Ettuthogai* and *Pathupattu*. It facilitated the dream of the Golden Era of the Tamils (vellalas). Though the same idea was used by poet Bharathi and Thiru.Vi. Ka as an anti-imperialistic weapon, what it really aided was the vellala revivalist argument. While in the hands of the vellalas, Tamil was being used for revivalism, simultaneously the stories, and news and essays that were carried by the new means of communication, the magazine, transformed the traditional relationship between the writer and the reader. The practice of writing different types of poems to please a patron or philanthropist in the tradition of conventional Tamil learning, ended. A new commercial practice appeared with the advent of a publisher who took on a writer, trying to reach a wider reading public. On its journey from the writer to the faceless reader, the writing passed through many centres created by heavy investment like printing press, paper, publishing house, advertisements, distributors, bookshops, textbooks and libraries. The educated brahmins were the ones who quickly took control of this system. Whether it was popular fiction in Tamil or highbrow literary works sought out by the intellectuals, the brahmins were the pioneers. The leadership of generations that has been in the hands of vellalas passed on to the brahmins.[7]

In the world of modern publications such as *Vivekachindamani* and *The Hindu* that were active in the ninteenth century, *Anandavikatan* of S. S. Vasan and Ramaswamy Krishnamurthy who wrote under the pen name Kalki, popular in the twentieth century, brahmins dominated. Kalki, who got wealth and fame through his popular writings, advertisement baron S. S. Vasan who amassed wealth through cinema, successful writers like Balakumaran, Sivasankari and Sujatha and the television actors are all brahmins. In short, wherever there is power, fame and wealth, there too the leading figures will be brahmins. The vellalas and other castes look upon brahmins as models. So far we have examined how the brahmins and the vellalas exercised power during different periods in the history of the Tamil country and how the bulk of the Tamil people who followed them, without any politics of their own, merely went behind those who dominated them.[8] To understand the problems of the present day, the people of Tamil Nadu should recognize the true face of the brahmins and the vellalas. It is my hope that this essay might help that process.

This chapter originally published in *Nirapirigai* Feb 1992; reprinted in *Dalit Vimarsana Katturaikal,* 2003, Kalachuvadu Publications, Nagercoil.

Notes

1   Ibn Batuta, *Travel Notes* http://www.columbia.edu/itc/mealac/pritchett/00generallinks/ibnbatuta/index.html; David Waines, *The Odyssey of Ibn Battuta: Uncommon Tales of a Medieval Adventurer* (London: I.B. Tauris, 2010).

2   Noboru Karashima, *South Indian History and Society: Studies from Inscriptions, A.D. 850–1800* (New Delhi: Oxford University Press, 1984).

3   A. Krishnaswami, *The Tamil Country under Vijayanagar* (Annamalainagar: Annamalai University, 1964.

4   Ma. Po. Sivagnanam, *Tamilnatil Piramoliyinar* (Chennai: Pulam Veliyeedu, 2009).

5   Arumuga Navalar, *Pirapantattirattu* (The Collected Works of the Noble and Venerable Arumuga Navalar), 3d ed. 2 vols. (Chennai:1954–55).

6   Mayilai Seeni Venkatasami, *Paththonpatham Nurrantil Tamil Ilakkiyam:* 1800–1900 (Chennai: Santi Nulakam, 1962).

7   Mathavaiya, A.. *Padmavati Charitram: A Story of the Tamil Country: Oru Tamilnattukkathai:* Muthal Pakam, Part I (Palghat: T. S. Subramania and Co.1898).

8   It is to be noticed in the history of the Tamil country, there was no varna called kshatriyas. The big landlords among vellalas, the Maravas and the Nayaks, were the commandants who performed the kshatriya work of governing.

5

Dravidian Literature:
Radical Features and Worldview

Mocking the Venerated

Mikhail Bakhtin said, 'Laughter is the antithesis of reverence'.[1] In a culture looked upon as solemn and held in high esteem, you will find embedded features like fear, weakness, suppression, ignorance, falsehood, violence, warning, threat, ban, censoring and deceit. These features construct authority. Bakhtin goes on to say that they wear a mask of deception. Mirth, gracelessness, parody, ridicule and derision have the muscle to tear this mask. Rollicking laughter will never be of help in suppressing people. It will never blind them. In fact, in the hands of the people this hilarity will function as a weapon. This gaiety of people, who have been subjugated by authoritarian, honoured, sacred and serious culture, liberates them from subjective as well as older and much deeper objective restrictions. It releases them from the fear of thousands of years relating to the sacred, the forbidden and authority. Bakhtin and others point out that only equals can laugh among themselves. If lower-caste, or lower-class, people laugh or are permitted to laugh in the presence of higher people, then the higher ones are likely to lose the respect they enjoyed. For instance, when, people are allowed to laugh in the presence of the Egyptian Bull-God Apis, the deity loses its sanctity and becomes an ordinary bull.

When the venerated is mocked by ordinary people, things reverse. Such mockery reduces the all-powerful into power-less and ordinary. The hallowed features of the venerated are removed. The bewildered ordinary people voicing for change are delighted. Self-respect and self-esteem replace guilt, fear, contrition and remorse. Feelings of community and harmony come to the fore.

In the protest of the oppressed who are at the bottom of society one can discern ridicule, parody, mockery, sarcasm and scorn. In folklore one can see how oppressed people ridicule members of the dominant caste who tyrannize over them. This has been reflected in printed literature also. In the 250-year-old Tamil work *Mukkoodarpallu*, the Pallar (Kudumbar) caste people make fun of their landlords. This kind of mockery is echoed in poet Bharathiyar's caricature of the zamindars. Echoes are found in A. Madhaviah's descriptions of deceitful brahmins. It can be seen in the bitter picture Pudumaipithan paints of urban life. The voice of feminists and black writers all over the world reverberate with such mockery. The writings of the Dravidian move-ment ideologues Periyar, Annadurai and Bharathidasan also reflect such a perspective.

In the Indian context, there is something in common between the ideas attacked by the Dravidians, dalits and women. All three of them target *Manusmiriti*, puranic ortho-doxy and patriarchical Brahminism. In other words, those who were subjected to criticism by Periyar were also targeted by dalits and feminists. In Periyar's discourse, feminism and dalit ideology have an indispensable place, even as he denigrates Brahminism and orthodox Hinduism with its varnasrama codes. The Dravidian ideologues saw them-selves as subjugated shudras (sons of whores), as Dravidians (linguistic group family) and as Tamils (nationals). In their writings they ridiculed and parodied the Vedas, chiefs of mutts, priests, the deities of the brahmins and puranic and epic characters. These are the sacred and honoured subjects in traditional literature. Dravidian literature started the practice of making fun of the sacred, honoured ideas and characters in Hindu culture. Earlier, long before, the siddhars, the Tamil mystics, who have left behind a corpus of poems, did this kind of ridiculing. But their aim was to reform things, within the religious context. The aim of spoofing in Dravidian literature was to demolish the Hindu religion and to capture the religion called political power.

In a short story titled 'The Job Is lost', C. N. Annadurai through some printing errors in a wedding invitation, ridiculed sanctities like vedic orthodoxy, priesthood and sanyasa. 'Swami Kavadiyananda' becomes 'Kami Savadiyananda' and 'Vedam' is printed as 'Bhetham'. These printing errors endow the words with the opposite meaning. Their original meaning is lost. When the words charged with respectability are made fun of, the connection between those words and authority is inversed, simultaneously liberating the minds of the suppressed, affording them emotional relief. This is the main function of rebel literature.

Even in naming the characters in his stories, Annadurai inverted propriety. Sanskrit names such as Bhuvaneswari, Kalyani, Damayanthi, Thilaka and Kokila are given to female deities and virtuous women. In his stories Annadurai had given these names that stand for divinity and sanctity to call girls. The wife of Hanumantha Rao, editor of a magazine called *Viyasar*, a character in the story 'The Job Is Lost' is named Sita. The assistant editor is named Garudazhvar. These names, Hanuman, Sita and Garuda are characters from the Vaishnavaite epic *Ramayanam.* Sita is the wife of Rama, the main protagonist of the epic. But in the story of Annadurai she is the wife of Hanuman, a factotum of Rama.

While Annnadurai used the names of the characters from the epic to tease, Bharathidasan went one step further and wrote a spoof of the epic itself. Titled *Revised Ramayana* it included a chapter called 'Telephone Episode' in which he employed terms like telephone and bathroom anachronistically to dilute the solemnity of the epic. Here is an extract.

It appeared Kaikeyi was in the bathroom.
Dasaratha walked towards the bathroom.
Which was circular with four entrances,
All the entrances were closed.
Dasaratha ran into Mr. Rama there
And was shocked and surprised.
'Rama, why did you come here?' he asked.
Rama answered that he came to see his step-mother.
'Did you plan to meet her in the bathroom?'
Asked Dasaratha.
'Why should you be so curious?' said Rama.
Dasaratha pleaded, 'Don't you love me, Rama?
Should you not look upon her as your step-mother?'
Rama grew angry!
'Though from the author's point of view
'Kaikeyi may be your wife
'and my step-mother
'But objectionable from the social norms of society.'

You can see that the celestial goings on are brought down to earth here. Note how Rama, the divine incarnation, talks to his father, Dasaratha, the king. The sanctity and honour of a noble family becomes the butt of ridicule. This is in fact a characteristic of folk tales.

Bharathidasan is at his satirical best when he writes about an encounter between Dasaratha and Manthara. When Dasaratha enraged on learning about Manthara's machinations screams at her, Manthara pulls a revolver from her waist and points it at him. Confronted with a revolver in the hands of a hunchbacked servant, the all-powerful king becomes powerless. The weapon becomes a symbol of rationalism, science and modernity. The sacred text loses its elevated meanings here. While concluding the story, Bharathidasan makes Kaikeyi challenge Rama and Dasaratha: 'Obey my command or try and resist these two Tamil women.' In the

Dravidian perspective, these two Tamil women (Kaikeyi and Manthara) defy patriarchy and Aryan headship. Rama and Ravana of the Aryan *Ramayana* get inverted in the epic of *Ravana Kaviyam*. Similarly, here Rama, Dasaratha, Kaikeyi and Manthara have been inverted. This feature is prominent in Dravidian rebel literature in which puranic characters beaten by brahminical supremacy such as Ravana, Iraniyan, Kumbakarna, Karnan, Duriyodanan and Manthara are endowed with contrasting, noble qualities. By this device the work of demolishing sublime ideologies at the conceptual and psychological level goes on.

Thus, Dravidian literature effectively trounced the official reverent and respected ideas through irreverent and unofficial means and exposed them. In the short story of Bharathidasan 'Blessing in a Whorehouse', two young men go seeking the blessing of a swamiji. Later, when they visit a brothel, they see the same swamiji there as a client. In another story of Bharathidasan titled 'Impediment to Reason', in a temple, the sanctum, the idol of Vishnu, and the Iyengar priest are all connected to a series of thefts. Gold and diamonds stolen by the priest are hidden inside the idol in the sanctum. Precisely those things viewed as honourable, dependable and respectable create fear, distrust and an inferiority complex among marginalized people. Bharathidasan's short stories throw light on the other side of these seemingly trustworthy and dependable features. The laughter provoked by this ridicule reveals a truth. More than that, experiencing this laughter and living through it is important. The aim of such lampooning is to break the unseen chains that bind the Dravidian people.

Of special importance is the story titled 'The Glory of God' in which Bharathidasan writes about how the menstrual period of a housewife comes in the way of fulfilling her sacred vow to cook and feed some priests. He places a pollution (menses) imagined by orthodoxy as against vedic ritual and mocks at it. Deriding sacred places, individuals and ceremonies through human excrescences like urine, menstrual discharge and shit, along with the use of scornful language is one feature of rebel literature. Subjugated people cannot fight ideas or attack with weapons. So they resort to a device whereby they use filthy language and terms that describe human excrescence, and use these words of filth and smut to find a way to escape from the lowliness of their birth. Bakhtin says that these are appropriate terms to de-sanctify the hallowed.[2] Bharathidasan pours scorn on a sacred ceremony by associating a woman's menstrual discharge with it. What is considered filth is brought into destroying the sanctity of a holy ritual. Simultaneously those affected by prejudice are renewed.

Only with the advent of Dravidian literature did prostitutes, thieves, mill workers, cart pullers, domestic servants, coolies and the poverty-stricken begin appearing in contemporary literary discourse. In the eyes of those who accepted only approved characters, these people appeared low, inefficient and degraded. These people and those who speak about them appear crazy, disruptive and disorderly. How did Periyar appear to Jawaharlal Nehru? In the eyes of the Congress brahmins of those days, Periyar, Annadurai, Karunanidhi and Bharathidasan appeared unruly, low-caste, subversive and disorderly individuals.

Those who stand up for high-brow literature saw the writings of these writers as inferior, labelling it low class, substandard and mere propaganda. They lamented that these writings were a stumbling block to the progress of Tamil and that Tamil literature was not able to reach great heights because of this. (This lament can still be heard.)

Literature also found a place along with the revered list of God, king, priest and *pathivirathai* (chaste woman) and was idolized and worshipped. In authoritative culture, each subject is categorized and arranged in a hierarchical order, with an ideal for each. But in the culture of those who oppose authoritative forms you will not find categorization.

Politics, culture, art and literature will all be mixed in their movement. Therefore you cannot compare rebel culture with authoritative culture. Rebel culture does not grow to be authoritative culture; it mocks idolized, highbrow literature and brings it down. It endows the unrecognized people with the power to create literature and energizes them. Highbrow literature is also an instrument of oppression. Just like Carnatic music, Bharathanatyam and Shakthi (female deity) worship, it has been idolized with rituals, ceremonies, gimmicks, sacred values, methods of censor and restrictions of Sastras. Rebel literature begins with the work of breaking this idol. The writers of the Dravidian movement have indulged in this iconoclastic work with restraint.

The rebel literature of the Dravidian movement is distinct. It is an amalgam of story, essay, forceful propaganda, violations, rule breaking, deconstructing language, the intrusion of the unaccepted, caricature, parody, intervention of the author, absurd descriptions, rude utterances, lack of realism and exaggeration. The people who shout that the Dravidian movement has harmed highbrow literature are the ones who support oppressive highbrow literature, the Vedas and Brahminism. But the Dravidian movement demonstrated that you can question accepted and authoritative positions and that such an act of protest is not a sin. In fact they created a kind of cultural celebration. Through their magazines, stories and essays they developed reading habits among dalits and other backward people. They converted commercial literature, which was fast becoming a consumer item, into rebel literature.

If one talks in praise of Dravidian literature as being of a high order and superior merely to counter brahminical criticism then that would be wrong. That will be making the same mistake that the retractors of Dravidian literature are making. In fact this is what happened after the Dravidian movement captured political power. Statements such as 'There is only one race and only one God', 'We see God in the smile of the poor', 'The jasmine in the neighbour's garden also will smell nice' and 'No need to demolish Ganesa temple nor is there any need to break coconuts' often mouthed by the Dravidian leaders are symbolic of the compromises they have made in their ideology. In the West, after the revolution, the Soviet government and the rule of the working class were carried on with the help of the old bureaucracy. Therefore it degraded and dissipated. In India, those who offer different excuses for the fall of the Soviet Union, trivialize the decline of the Dravidian movement. It is with revulsion that Congress brahmins look upon the backward castes and dalits of the Dravidian movement. Consciously and unconsciously this Sanathana perspective looks negatively at the Dravidian movement, government and literature.

The Dravidian writers, pouring scorn, turned on their heads the ideas held as sublime by the establishment, extended it by doing something else. They accepted the very things that the establishment looked upon as repulsive, distasteful and nauseating and by rebelling against it in their personal lives, ripped off its mask. This kind of exposure is one dimension of the literature of revolt. Annadurai achieves this through the short story 'A Clerk's Daughter'.

In this story Kantha, a young daughter of a brahmin clerk watches a play titled 'A Clerk's Daughter'. The heroine of the play, Sita, because of the poverty at home, is married to an old brahmin who dies soon after their wedding. Sita suffers all the indignities of a young widow. Like the heroine of the play, Kantha also becomes a young widow. When her relatives come one after another and advise Kantha how to conduct her life, she laments

> None came forward to help us when we were in want.
> No one was interested in getting me married to a suitable man.
> As my life was ruined, no one took notice.
> In the end, when I became a widow, relatives
> Came to advise me on how to conduct myself as a widow.
> Their only concern was that the family honour should be intact.

My home is a prison to me. My father, mother
Are the guards. My relatives are the police and
The village folks are the judges who convict me.

When a landlord tries to molest her, Sita takes her own life. Through the affected young woman Annadurai establishes how authoritative systems such as the prison, police and judges function through advice, warning and punishment. In addition to the ideological violence of family honour, parents, and social mores, Annadurai adds direct sources of violence like prison, police and courts.

Kantha, the heroine of Annadurai's story, did not kill herself like Sita did in the play. Instead she became the mistress of Vedagiri Mudaliar who was enamoured of her. Then she declares war on the society that had been hostile to her. Annadurai's device of appropriating a character shunned in the play is the critical factor of rebel literature. It can be considered a war against a hegemonic world that consists of prison-family, guards-parents, police-relatives and judges-people of the village.

Those who are projected as civilized, sophisticated, law-abiding gentlemen, capitalists, impartial observers, honest folks and respected citizens are the ones who are behind this organized oppression. To preach that they are the ones who elevate the suppressed is to keep the suppressed forever under servitude. If they say that suppressed people are responsible for their own condition that would be a device to get them used to that repressed state. To label resistance to tyrannical laws and through revolutionary action to counter violent unlawful acts, they criminalize even the oppressed people's attempts at liberation. Most people cannot see through this magic of the ideological scheme. On the other hand, in order to bring about a change we have to examine what has so far been described as sinful, criminal, inappropriate, and wrong. One has to look again at what is accepted as 'proper' behaviour. A different set of social mores may become necessary to work out strategies against hegemonic culture and to move towards alternative life patterns. Pretending to be respectful, parodying behind the back, failing to keep one's given word, pretending to be insane and violating other standards may be resorted to. If the horse is to get rid of its burden, it has to throw off its rider and not obey his commands.

Kantha, the protagonist in the short story of Annadurai, chooses and enters such a life of struggle. She becomes the mistress of a landlord and wins his affection. She makes him wait on her like a dog. No one in the village dares raise his voice against her. Judges, police and prison officials are all silent. Finally, when her old lover comes to murder her, she kills him. In Kantha's chosen life, instead of going through the accepted sufferings of a widow and eventually committing suicide, she resorts to murder. Instead of getting penalized by long-established custom, Kantha turns around and overpowers tradition. That is the only way to organize an alternate life. Because she is a woman, her sexual conduct is widely noticed.

Though Annadurai's purpose is to expose the chicanery of brahmins, since the story is from the point of view of the subjugated, the features of rebel literature blossom here. A widow choosing to be a mistress and thus breaking the code held as sublime is an act of revolt. Similarly exposing those who propagate such discipline as being hollow and false is also an act of rebellion. This device is used frequently in Dravidian literature. This is different from ridiculing ideas through parody. What is accepted as standard morality is in fact utterly shallow.

The Binary Opposites in Dravidian Literature

In Dravidian literature we see opposites such as town *vs.* village, capitalist *vs.* labourer, rich *vs.* poor, brahmin *vs.* shudra and Aryan *vs.* Dravidian. In these sets of opposites, the category appearing first is in a higher position than the second. However, the one in a higher place does not deserve that position any more than the one in the lower spot. In fact, those in the lower position have been artificially positioned to appear superior to those in the higher place. This is reflected even in the manner in which the characters have been named. The higher—evil ones—have brahminic-Sanskrit names, and the innocent ones in the lower positions bear Tamil names. The naming pattern in the writing of Dravidian writer Mu.Varadarasan is a good example.

Dravidian literature depicts (town) capitalist, rich man, brahmin and Aryan as exploiting; the (village) the worker, poor man, shudra and Dravidian. Bharathidasan uses the word 'Tamilian' as opposed to brahmin. However, the literature of the Dravidian movement does not draw attention to caste while dealing with the graded society. One particularly notices that the caste identities of dalits, who are crushed under untouchability, are overlooked. In one short story Bharathidasan used Dravidian terminology and referred to dalits as 'Adi Dravidas'. Even among shudras, two categories are listed. Though all non-brahmins are considered shudras, there is a division between higher and lower shudras. Adi Dravidas are grouped separately. The upper-caste shudras are comfortably pigeon-holed as Mudaliar, Pillai and Reddy. Thevar and Nayudu who are on the upwardly mobile move are also mentioned. But the names of lower rung shudra castes are not mentioned. Instead they are given different rubrics: inhabitants of slums, farmhands, millworkers and poor folks. Saivite Tamil names and secular names such as Velappan, Kandhan, Sokkan, Ponni, Thangam, and Irulappan can also be seen in Dravidian literature. What is the reason for this? The voices raised against brahminic hegemony were varied. These voices were not uniform like those of the brahmins. This is because the non-brahmin castes were categorized in a hierarchical order as vellala castes, advanced backward castes and dalits. This pluralistic hierarchy gives power to the brahmin minority and weakens the majority non-brahmin. In fact, the majority in this context is an amalgam of minorities. The vellala castes talked about the glory of Tamil and about Saivisim. The bulk of the backward castes and vellalas gathered under the leadership of Periyar and talked about Dravidian ideas, self-respect, atheism, rationalism and the liberation of shudras; they also talked about the pride of being a Tamil. Some of the educated pariahs who were with them, under the name Adi Dravida, talked about the liberation of the untouchables. Many vellalas believed in Periyar's ideas and they accepted his anti-brahmin stand.

Though all these polyphonic voices could create an emotional unity, they could not fashion a majoritarian force out of the many castes that functioned below the brahmins. Such a force could probably be created by abolishing caste. While nursing caste diversities, they ignored the differences among them, pretending that they did not exist. Emotionally charged labels such as Tamil, Tamil race, shudra, self-respect, worker, poor, Dravidian and Adi Dravida came in handy. Without eradicating caste, the minority brahmin caste hegemony could not be shaken till today. Mere attempts to hide caste variations and contradictions within rubrics like Tamilian, shudra, Dravidian and Adi Dravida have proved futile. Moreover after the Dravidian movement captured political power decades ago in 1967, people of the vellala caste acquired considerable power. Backward-caste people (middle-level castes) who progressed and who acquired some wealth have a considerable number of positions in politics, among academics, in the bureaucracy and the police. Their position is much better in Tamil Nadu than in many other states in India. Still, whenever dalits try to enjoy the benefits of these changes, middle-level caste people continue to attack and try to destroy them, in a manner much more demonic than the brahmin-vellala combine. Those who have benefitted from Dravidian movements outdo the brahmins and vellalas in their efforts to crush the dalits. In this respect, the Dravidian movement has been a big disappointment for dalits. It has established the need for a separate dalit liberation movement.

Instead of looking upon brahmins as adversaries, one has to challenge the caste structure that is forcing varna-srama dharma, untouchability, patriarchy, vedic culture and Hindutva ideology on people. The people who aim to pull down the hegemony of the caste above them, should consider castes below them as equal. (Is this feasible at all?) We should be a society that has differences other than those that are caste-based. (This is nice to hear.) But these differences should not bring about inequalities. In such a situation there will no place for a brahmin caste. When many castes keep fighting among themselves, brahmins as a solid caste, though small in number, will continue to be in a dominating position. Any caste that acquires property and power will be hegemonic like the brahmin caste. It will behave like the brahmin caste. Whoever tries to pull down brahmins, and become brahmin themselves will turn out to be more cruel than the brahmins themselves. This can be observed even now.

The Worldview of the Dravidian Movement

It is clearly expressed through the literature of the Dravidian movement that its worldview is the demolition of the supremacy of brahmins. In this effort, the rationalist, and atheist, romanticist, and socialist points of view are combined. This can be observed in Annadurai's praise of Columbus for his adventurous voyage and Bharathidasan's derision of Rasputin of Russia. Columbus stands like a symbol of individual achievement, freedom, economic ideology and progress. In the Tamil context he is projected as a representation of Tamil, Dravidian and shudra. The deceitful priest Rasputin stands for brahminic authority. In the person of Rasputin the qualities of Aryan, brahmin, vedic orthodoxy, Sanathana ideology, capitalists and the wealthy are combined.

The last part of a short story entitled 'Rationlist Proscription' by Bharathidasan takes the form of an essay.

> People of India never tried to examine the nature of the
> five elements of earth. Instead they became the servants
> of these elements. However, the wonders of our modern
> world such as telegraph, railway and television have been
> realized by researching these five and by gaining control
> over them.

In these words that welcome the achievement of science one
can also observe the atheistic ideas of the bourgeoisie. In the
place vacated by God, things and properties replace human
beings. It can be recalled that this attitude reflects the
bourgeois view which brought down feudalism in the West.
This is also the perspective of the Dravidian movement. This
view has empowered the movement to bring down brahminic
orthodoxy. It is against this background that the Dravidian
movement supported the English language and the scientific
knowledge that can be gained through it. Periyar once went
to the extent of saying that all Tamilians should accept
English as their mother tongue.

The atheistic rationalist outlook and the romanticist
socialist point of view are combined to benefit vellala and
developed backward castes and economically backward
castes respectively. The vellala caste leadership was growing
into small and big capitalists even as it questioned the supremacy of the brahmins, and harnessed romantic socialism as
an instrument to collect the the working class under them.
Rarely are brahmin capitalists depicted as adversaries in
Dravidian literature. Instead they are portrayed as archaic
zamindars or landlords.

To hide the internal paradoxes among the non-brahmin
castes some fabrications were deployed as also romantic socialism. The true intention of the vellala and forward caste leadership of the Dravidian movement became clear after they
captured governmental power and began taking a neutral and
noncommital stand with regard to contradictions like piety,
atheism, capitalism and the working class.

Paper read in a seminar on Dravidian literature in Hosur in April 1994. Revised for publication in the journal *Nirapirigai* October 1995). Subsequently republished in *Poy+Abatham=Unmai* Vidiyal Pathippagam, Coimbatore. 2001.

Notes

1   Michael Bakhtin, *Rabelais and His World* (Indianapolis: Indiana University Press, 2009).
2   Ibid.: 151–52.

6

Postmodernism and Dalit Ideology

THE HUMAN SUBJECT; the existence of arbitrariness between word and meaning; ideological construction; historical truth; new power relations; there is no centre; multi-faceted nature; many possibilities about reality; removing those which become like natural; forms of protests by marginalized people; the new concepts proclaiming that there are no common final incomparable truths that have been subjected to rigorous examination. This has gone further in the West by thinkers like Nietzsche, Stephen Greenblatt, Michel Foucault, and others towards postmodernism. I have identified the ideas listed above for the sake of this study of dalit inquiry. It is not an exhaustive list of the concepts contained in postmodernism thinking. Moreover, postmodernism has many voices and many striking branches.

Let us begin with the view of Ferdinand de Saussure on linguistic signs and then move towards the growth of postmodernism. Saussure's primary aspect is about language. To him language is above all, a structure: this structure has rules and regulations (or internal grammar). These interact with various aspects of language. A linguistic sign comprises of two parts, the signifier and the signified. The signifier is sound, and the signified is word concept. In the language there are only differences, no positive terms.[1] The relation between the signifier and signified is quite arbitrary. The value of a sign is produced by the differences between words.

We create something in addition to what is already there. The content of a signified sign is not a thing to be found in the world. That is a linguistic relationship. In other words this is a description of a sign. It does not start from reality. To put it in other words, it is not to fix a meaning of the words in a reality which is beyond linguistics.

The arbitrariness between the words and meaning eventually becomes a convention and gets naturalized, that is, the relationship between signifier and signified is arbitrary. Scholars say that the idea that the representing ability of signs is arbitrary has been used by semiotics in cinema and culture studies. Dalit ideologues should remember that this arbitrariness is not inherent or inseparable and is not a permanent part of a sign. It has a political significance.

It points out that if they want to and if they try, dalits can also play with the meaning of signs. In the mind of the dalit, used to tradition and blunted by it, the possibility of re-examination is planted. In the Indian, Tamil Nadu contexts, traditional cultural images and signs reflect caste implications. Today the arbitrariness of signs helps dalits to question the relation between caste connotation and signs. It is possible to trace caste implications (which have become like a permanent feature) to its origin and expose it as being hollow and fragile.

Postmodernism subjects to scrutiny what is generally accepted as 'proper', 'normal' and 'common'. 'Normal' denotes something permanent, that which exists forever, that which precedes language and is the centre. This centre which transcends time and place is like a being and like the divine being. But of course there is no such centre. Jacques Derrida referred to this metaphysical belief in this non-existent centre as logocentrism. It is believed that this centre, which is not there, decides meanings and that this rational principle that acts as the centre exerts control over matters related to the external world. Derrida rejects this on a philosophical basis. For him there is no such implicit rational principle. It is all a mere illusion. Time and place change and all that is related to them too change. But the centre we are referring to is seen as unchanging, surpassing time and place. Postmodernism deconstructs this concept of the centre.

No outfit is harmonious or finalized. Derrida says it is the belief in logocentricism which makes most people think that it is harmonious; makes them long for such complete outfits and find satisfaction in that concept. He refers to it as 'the intense passion for the lasting truth that transcends history'. Because of this passion, culture, religion, ethics, piety and related rituals in our caste-based culture have been celebrated as sacred, unblemished and worthy of preservation.

Bakthin explains, 'There is no first word or final word. All the myriad meanings in History are constructed by the struggle between the forces of daily life.'[2] Tamil writer Puthumaipithan (1906–1948) echoes this when he wrote 'life is boundless. God has not written the last page of life yet. Even for him it would be an impossible task. Life is not bound even by justice.'[3]

Beliefs in rationalist principle, permanent centre, harmony and the finalized mystify many issues. These beliefs have justified caste structure, factors that facilitate it and the discourse related to it as normal, intellectual and harmonious. From the Vedas, Sanathanic principle, Dharmasastras to the present-day political constitution, merit, skill, hardwork and growth, everything makes the dalit blind to what is his or her own. Postmodernism emphasizes the need to deconstruct these factors. The deconstruction work that the dalit embarks on, projects him as a radical in the political and economic plane. In Tamil Nadu E. V. Ramasami Periyar has already demonstrated this.[4] Since postmodernism provides a strong theoretical background to this discourse dalits cannot be written off so easily.

Modern inanities such as 'there is no caste, we should not talk about hierarchy by birth, should not discriminate on caste' are often acclaimed as progressive positions. On the other hand, these statements adapt caste to modern times; make it appear normal as if everyone agrees with this position. It is postmodernism which makes us realize that what appears normal is in fact dangerous to the dalits. So we have to pare it to the minimum and examine what is projected as normal. When we examine the statement that there is no caste and no high or low, you will find the connotation that there *is* caste, there *is* grading but we should not mind it. What is lurking behind such an attitude is the view that to talk about existence of caste is uncivilized, backward and not modern.

The traditional brahminic trading castes and contemporary bourgeoisie forces have constructed the deception that all that is happening is normal and is accepted by all. It is the historic duty of dalits and other marginalized folks to deconstruct these two forces and uncover their true face. In the West it was Nietzsche who deconstructed ethics. It was the bourgeoisie that projected human rights, humanitarianism and human nature as modern ethics. And Roland Barthes deconstructed these modern myths and examined their hegemonic significance.

We will have to examine how dalits construct their own discourse based on history and deconstruct other concepts. To get an answer to this question we turn to Lévi-Strauss. His idea on the engineering skills of primitive people is called 'Bricolage'.[5] Derrida also uses this concept in his discussions on 'Bricolage'.[6] He compares the attempt to elevate oneself by creating a discourse out of history to a primitive craftsman creating a handicraft out of what is left of making another artifact. Usually we begin our discussion from 'readymade' concepts. They have been formed at a different time for a different purpose.

Derrida points out that we modify them to suit what we are doing now and that all thoughts are like Bricolage. Through Derrida, dalits can acquire a new intellectual methodology. A dalit can deconstruct what has been denied to him as untouchable and what has been created for oppressions and modify them as new discourse to be used for his own elevation and for the elimination of caste. In this way all thoughts of ours are of Bricolage. Dalits can *only* refashion what is available and use it to get through the present predicament. Postmodernism did not supply a political ideology. It provides a method to break what we are used to in history. We can say that it provides an epistemology to facilitate our political-economic struggle. It can also come in handy in the struggles related to art and literature. The dalit discourse in Tamil Nadu today differs from similar discourse in Marathi or Kannada. Like modern feminism, today modern dalit discourse can absorb and use insights from modernity. In Tamil Nadu today, from among the non-dalit intellectuals, some leftist thinkers and some influenced by postmodernism have become supporters of dalits and reject caste. It is doubtful if this development would have taken place without the idea of postmodernist thinking.

Let us now examine what the dalits can write about, speak on, what their alternative power discourse is and how to start a dialogue with those in authority. 'Those start actively to "write" themselves upon the structure, will continue as a product on this structure'. Michel Foucault explains the connection between constructing an authority and generating truth. He says: 'It is not enough to speak the truth. One has to be within the truth to speak the truth.' He goes on to add,

> More than anything else, speaking is to possess the authority to speak. Speech is discourse and there is a connection between authority and discourse. Capturing power also means appropriating the discourse. So the aim of the struggle for authority is discourse. The exercise of authority is continuously setting up new intellectual activities and targets. And these establish a specific method of authority.[7]

Dalits who were not allowed to speak have to gain the authority to speak in the first place. The liberation of dalits is tied up with the annihilation of the caste system. So to destroy the power of caste, dalits have to construct an alternate discourse and a different authority. Intellectual discourse is basically a discourse of authority. Therefore it is clear how urgent, difficult and necessary it is to construct it.

Bakthin says that those who have been denied speech should begin a 'dialogue' with the dominant/official forces. You have to begin by facing the authoritative factors squarely, subject them to parody and subvert the existing methods in the beginning.[8] In other words, dalits have to begin the dialogue by subversion against oppression, through subversive behaviour, speech, gesture, laughter and day-to-day practices. The logical end of this process will be unrest. On the other hand, it might fail to produce any such result. It can end up being a mere antic or temporary violation without creating any impact. It might also end up in a revolution.

Let us now quickly look at what Foucault says about history, growth (development), unity, continuity and hegemonic construction and also at the criticism against Foucault.[9] History is progressive without a break; it is only out of necessity that everything happens in history. Foucault's study rejects the traditional idea that history has a grand beginning. History is neither planned nor continuous as humans think. It can be recalled that Marx said 'human beings create their own history; but not as they want it to be'. Humans can never comprehend history, as it is, objectively. If they wish to understand history in that manner they should position themselves outside history, outside time. Only 'God' can be in that position. But that 'God' cannot talk to us. Therefore according to postmodernism there can be no such thing as history from outside. Postmodernism concludes that all these ideas are constructed through ideology, language and through the positions human beings take. Such an idea of history tells us how to approach history and what position we should take. Vedic religious culture has fabricated that in the external world and in the life of each being history is revolving like a wheel. The ideas of postmodernism help to bring down these fabrications easily.

Further, we will see that Foucault's postmodernist observations on history and growth help in providing justice to dalits. Foucault demolishes the customary mental practice of bringing scattered incidents into a regulated method through the principle of order into the system of cause and effect and to see growth as a continuous process. Due to this view of growth, dalits and other aborigines are ridiculed as having moved away from a civilized life struggle and become resigned to a backward position. The dominant forces think that these people should be helped with rehabilitation programmes to bring them on par with the other castes. Foucault's critique provides the dalits with an argument to oppose such official 'development programmes'. Conservative Marxists and leftist thinkers also agree with this plan for 'development'. D. D. Kosambi is a good example of such thinking. Explaining the reason for the backwardness of tribal people Kosambi says that they live in remote areas untouched by civilization, bound by superstitions, rituals and out of date practices that prevent them from trying any new methods. In other words he says that they are the reason for their own backwardness. He traces the history of low-caste origins from tribals.[10] This is in fact the collective conclusion of upper castes. Whether it is leftist, centrist or rightist thinkers, their conclusions are the same.

Foucault questioned this kind of thinking. 'There is no need for your history to decide our growth. We will decide about our growth. Our view of growth is different.' Questions like what growth is, and who decides it, are important. After destroying dalits, a part of a major human force, for the sake of the growth of a civilization based on ownership, it is meaningless to talk about the development that the dalits have to undertake to reach this civilization; it is about unbearable violence.

Hegemonic forces, in order to safeguard their authority, conform to categorization and continuation of the marginalized class and categorize people on the basis of gender, economics, race, skin colour and food. Dalits have been categorized as lower class on the basis of birth and untouchability. The dalits according to the official method of unity are relegated to the margins. On the basis of continuous cause-effect, the logic for their existence is uttered. Therefore intervening and destroying the act of categorization and the logic of continuity is tantamount to destroying caste domination and its history.

Foucault explains how in civilized society marginalized people were pushed to the edge and the methods by which they were neglected. Hegemonic culture attributes differences to the opposite forces and thereby defines itself. Then, it castigates the polarizing point it has created through purification ceremonies, classifying rituals and ostracizing rituals. It strikes dumb those in the opposite camp. This hegemonic culture declares that those within its definition of 'truth' are normal and those outside are demons. Writing about authority in another context, Foucault defines human subjectivity by two reactions to authority: submitting to authority and opposing it. Similarly he defines the two dimensions of authority: enforcing and acquiescing to authority. Postmodern ideologue E. T. Bannet criticizes this simple explanation of Foucault. She says that Foucault ignores possibilities other than these two approaches that decide subjective positions and two kinds of relations.[11] This is worth keeping in mind.

This is a problem arising out of dividing society into binary opposites. We have to take note that in the Tamil Nadu context, in the binary opposites that Foucault used, there is no space for dalits. Foucault's detailed explanation about the management infrastructure for enforcing authority rejects multidimension. Foucault's explanation does not touch class, race or criminal tradition. There is no separate voice or convention for those in these categories. Other than what has been forced on them by the technology of authority they do not have anything of their own. It seems they do not have the skill to live in a different cultural context. Bannet's

criticism points out that Foucault's explanation is the cause
of the above contradictory matter.[12] This criticism cautions
that postmodern ideas should be approached critically by
everyone, including dalits.

The reality and truth of life in this world are not viewed
in the same way by everyone but have multiple possibilities.
Postmodernism shows that a variety of subjective interpretations are possible. We first have to examine Bakthin's
ideas about polylogue (any living language that is constantly
changing with words developing as the need arises). He is a
pioneer in this line of thinking. We can begin the enquiry
from the point where Bakthin says that there are differing
realities. Bakhtin writes:

> You can see what is behind my back. But I cannot see
> that. I can see what is behind your back and what has
> been hidden from your view. Though we are doing the
> same thing, we do that from two different points of
> view. Though we are involved in the same occurrence, it
> appears different to us. Our bodies may be functioning
> in different planes but our places do not differ. Our
> places differ because we see this world and each other
> from different centres.[13]

Bakthin points out that the reality we try to create, to understand, grows dissimilar. This is because often the event is one,
but the places are different, the action is one but the centres
of time and space are varied. So Bakthin stresses what we try
to create and give recognition to are different from reality.
We can trace the growth of this idea in 'Theory on the
Possible Worlds' introduced by Bannet. Marxism states that
words, texts and discourses reflect the truth. But postmodernism rejects this. These do not reflect either life, world, reality
or history. Instead they intrude. Postmodernism denies the
stand of Marxism that truth is embedded in history, in discourse and in text. Bannet says 'Marxism states that there
is only one rationalization for society and culture. Marxist

framework holds that only one kind of explanation is the correct one and that all the others are all wrong.[14] It says, on moral grounds, this is what will eventually unfold.' Bannet points to this as one specific kind of explanation and says all the others are wrong. But 'Theory on the Possible Worlds' 'rejects such one-dimensional explanations and holds that there are many possible worlds'. According to this position there have always been many possibilities that humans were not aware of. It is impossible to understand the world totally. One cannot understand it externally. Therefore it is impossible to have a single explanation, a single reality and a single truth. There are many possible realities, many worlds and many truths. Bannet points out that fictional stories in literature are all about possible worlds.[15]

The possible worlds can be true and at the same time include those that are untrue.[16] The real world can be looked at as one of the many possibilities. Therefore it is clear that these many possibilities coexist. And one of these may be the true possibility.[17] This way postmodernist ideas open up wide-ranging possibilities for the aesthetic, political and social movements of dalits. It appears that the world of caste can also be one of the possibilities. But this has been taken as the real world and people have interacted with it. It might have been true at one point of time. Probably there were no other possibilities. But will it continue like this? In history what has been seen as a fact is later proved to be fiction and something seen as fiction has turned out to be factual. So there is a chance that the real possibility of a casteist society might become fiction.

Marxism holds that revolution, leadership by working class and classless society, could contribute to the political struggle of dalits. This can be evaluated through the criticism of postmodernism against the European bourgeoisie, workers and revolution. Bannet said about the Marxist framework,

> The whole history is decided by a preconceived future. In other words, it leads towards a future of a classless society

and a working class revolution. It is in the future that the
desired change is expected. Such a view of the future,
authenticates a particular kind of reading of the past
(history). According to the official reading of Marxism,
classes that dominated society at different points in
history, were overthrown through revolution by the classes
oppressed by them.[18]

She goes on to say 'the main aim of history is to move towards
a classless society through revolution. In such a framework,
the future explains the past. And the past explains the future.
In the middle of the two, the present appears like a gate
between the old and the new.[19] This observation seems to
contrast the Marxian infrastructure with the Indian religious
view of the present life as an entry point from birth to re-birth.
One can thus understand how Marxism can co-exist with
Indian society that is steeped in caste and religious beliefs.
One can be a caste or a religious fanatic and yet be a Marxist
and be a part of the Communist Party. Postmodernism helps
the dalit realize that the reason for this situation is within
Marxist infrastructure. The classes that have been oppressed
have risen against the hegemonic class and have won in a
series of confrontations. This process has helped in the
growth of civilization. Following this development, logically,
the working class would overthrow the bourgeoisie through
revolution and bring about an ideal classless society. But
there are problematic questions such as what is the working
class doing now? In this context the break up of the Soviet
Union appears as an example.

The observations of Bannet and Jean Baudrillard on what
the working class has been doing and is doing in Europe
can annoy traditional Marxists. Let us first look at Bannet's
criticism.

A large part of the European working classes attached
themselves to Fascism first and later to Protestant trade
unions. Then they joined the radical politics of 'marginal people' like students, women and racial minorities.

Observing these changes postmodernist and post- Marxist thinkers came to the conclusion that they can no longer expect revolution from the working classes. Revolution is very likely to emerge from different groups of marginalized peoples. These groups came to the conclusion that by consulting each other jointly or through a kind of democratic management alliance, revolution can appear.[20]

We can examine the position of Tamil Nadu dalits against the background of this observation. Though they should be in the category of the working class, because of the practice of untouchability, degradation, denial of rights and with a distinct history of their own, dalits have been pushed to the 'margin' and are living as a sub-cultural group. Unless they find a solution that can redeem them from their marginalized position, they cannot dream of a classless society in the future. Marx described religion as the opium of the masses. Similarly the idea of a classless society is proffered to the dalits like opium. Dalits have also learnt a few lessons about the class struggle. Bannet writes as from experience: 'The centralized planning that Marx and Lenin advocated could be used for suppression. It could create a dictator: or create a new hegemonic class or technocrat class. It will not create a classless society.'[21]

Next we come to what Baudrillard has to say about the European bourgeoisie, the working class and revolution. He points out that

In Europe, the working class has never been a class. The real class was the bourgeoisie. The classless society that was to appear after the revolution never came into being. But the bourgeoisie along with capitalism denied itself and in the process has created a classless society. But there is no connection between this and the classless society that was expected after the revolution of the proletariat. Both the class struggle and the working class have disappeared without a trace. If capitalism had grown with its internal contradictions, it would certainly have been wrecked by the working class. Instead, capitalism grew alert. To avoid the danger to its very existence, it politicized itself transcending time and place. It centred itself at a point beyond political contradictions. By doing this it floated freely without any particular form or shape. It made itself free and unattached to anything. It also shaped this world in its own form.[22]

Baudrillard's observation points out that in the West not only has the working class been destroyed, but also because of different situations, the bourgeoisie, the world, the environment and the human race are getting devastated. Traditional Marxists oppose postmodernism, without properly examining it or it is due to political reasons. British literary theorist T. F. Eagleton hits out particularly strongly.

> Postmodernism represents bourgeoisie culture. It takes revenge on revolutionary forces and ridicules them. It empties the political content of modernism. Its culture is shallow and lacks finesse. It erases history and mocks socialism. The reason is that Nietzscheism is the philosophical basis of this. Anarchy is the only revolution possible through this ideology. 'Revolution' and 'Anarchy' are used like synonyms. The criticism of traditional Marxists, wherever they are, is also similar.[23]

Today, the new incarnations of the bourgeoisie have also engulfed the societies of Third World countries, and the instruments of mass communications facilitate this process. In this situation, dalits will not shed their caste indignity by merging with the 'proletariat'. There is no convincing excuse for the dalits to carry on a discourse on the class plane. Moreover, will dalits be allowed to carry on such an exchange of ideas? But it is clear that dalits are needed for the working class to have a dialogue with the bourgeoisie. In Indian caste culture, whether it is the bourgeoisie or the proletariat, the dalits are looked down upon or are not considered human beings at all. Capitalism which modernized India, steeped in traditional culture, has done that in accordance with the caste hierarchy. Therefore dalits should take into consideration the criticism by postmodernism against class struggle and revolution.

Postmodernism has to be accepted critically. Solutions and analysis that suit a particular place and specific problems relating to society may not be acceptable in another place, time and society. Some of the perceptions of postmodernism can be helpful for the dalits to redeem their place and give a fillip to their activity of knowing, analysing and destroying.

Paper presented at Manonmaniam Sundaranar University, Tirunelveli, November 1997.

Notes

1 F.de Saussure, *Course in General Linguistics*, trans and annotated by Roy Harris (London: Duckworth, 1983): 118.

2 M. M. Bakhtin, *The Dialogic Imagination: Four Essays* (Austin: University of Texas Press, 1983): 39.

3 Puthumaipithan, '*Kayitraravam*' short story in *Pudumaipithan Siru-kathaikal,* Mee.Pa. Somasundaram, ed. (New Delhi: NBT,.1976).

4 Periyar, E, V. Ramasami Naicker, '*Why Caste Should Be Ended*', Veeramani, ed., pamphlet, 1996.

5 C. Lévi-Strauss, *The Savage Mind* (Chicago: University of Chicago Press, 1966).

6 J. Derrida, *Writing and Difference*, trans Alan Bass (Chicago: University of Chicago Press, 1978): Chapter 10.

7 Eve Tavor Bannet, *Postcultural Theory: Cultural Theory after the Marxist Paradigm* (New York: Palgrave Macmillan, 1993).

8 Bakhtin, *The Dialogic Imagination: Four Essays*; M. Holquist, *Dialogism: Bakhtin and His World* (New York: Routledge, 1993).

9 Bannet, *Postcultural Theory: Cultural Theory after the Marxist Paradigm.*

10 D. D. Kosambi, *Myth and Reality: Studies in the Formation of Indian Culture* (Mumbai: Popular Prakashan, 1962); *The Culture and Civilisation of Ancient India in Historical Outline* [1965] (New Delhi: Vikas 1994); Vasudha Dhagamwar, *Role and Image of Law: The Tribal Experience.* (New Delhi: Sage, 2006).

11 Bannet, *Post-Cultural Theory: Critical Theory after the Marxist Paradigm.*

12 Ibid.: 39.

13 Bakhtin, *Dialogic Imagination*: 21

14 Bannet, *Post-Cultural Theory*: 1–22.
15 Ibid.: 117.
16 Ibid.: 120.
17 Ibid.: 122.
18 Ibid.: 18.
19 Ibid.
20 Ibid.: 19.
21 Ibid.: 19–20.
22 Jean Baudrillard, *The Transparency of Evil: Essay on Extreme Phenomena*, Trans. James Benedict (London: Verso, 1993).
23 T. F Eagleton, *The Crisis of Contemporary Cultures* (Oxford: Clarendon Press. 1993).

7

From the Subaltern Perspective: Re-Examination and Social Transformation

IT WAS THE Italian Marxist Antonio Gramsci (1881–1937) who first used the word 'subaltern' in a political context. This includes Subaltern Studies, research on marginalized people and their history. The discourse on Subaltern Studies brings up the names of Marx-Engels, Iyothee Thass, Dr. Ambedkar, and E. V. Ramasami Periyar. However, the most important among them all is Ranajit Guha who from 1960 onwards has been working on this subject and has brought out a series of important works.

In this essay I would like to briefly discuss three points: (*i*) Who are the subalterns? (*ii*) What is their history? (*iii*) From their perspective what needs to be done for a social transformation?

I

The usual meaning given for the term 'subaltern' is marginalized people or people relegated to the fringe: specifically people who are downgraded on the basis of race, gender, caste, and tribe. In other words, the term is used to refer to people discounted or disregarded by what dominant history has spun so far. The phrase 'disregarded people' would include tribals and 'untouchable' dalits and women. In recent years some non-dalits have made a long list of marginalized people for the purposes of propaganda. This includes lesbians, gays, bisexuals, transgenders, drug addicts, alcoholics and the mentally ill, criminals, and so on.

Bulgarian-French feminist linguist Julia Kristeva said in terms of linguistic, symbolic discipline and society, women are marginalized people.[1] In the concept of the 'subaltern' that Kristeva put forward there was no examination of social relations.

Though the working class is central to production, the owners of the means of production and powerful castes have kept them on the margins. Hill people and dalits are the key factors in production but in the political, economic and cultural context have been pushed to the edge of the society. Similarly, women occupy a central place in economic and human reproduction. But the strength of patriarchy has sidelined them culturally and politically. It is clear that tribal people, dalits and women have been contained on the fringes though their place in production is central. The main reason for being pushed to the periphery is their birth. Because the stamp of untouchability and gender comes with birth, these people have been relegated to the edge. They have a duty to change this state of affairs through revolutionary methods. Except for the transgenders, others who have been relegated to the margin, such as junkies, gamblers, thieves are not handicapped by birth. This has to be clearly understood. By the rehabilitation programmes of government and non-governmental organizations they can be restored to their position in society. In all societies one can identify such people. They do not have a role in the production process. We have to bear these limitations in mind when we deal with the problems of the marginalized.

In India and other South Asian countries, the concept of Subaltern Studies took shape while researching anti-colonial struggles in postcolonial years. It informed the study of the nature and methods of the struggles of the subaltern. In India, particularly, the idea of liberation, and the political and social transformation from the point of view of the mass of marginalized people like tribal people in the hill areas, women and dalits became subjects of study.

In history, the world over, the primary transformation was the shift from tribal society to agricultural society. This important social makeover that history records is the beginning of human civilization or ownership civilization. Consequent to this change in tribal societies a lot of differences and contradictions appeared. Specifically these differences arose and operated on the basis of gender, ownership of property, language, age, vocation and race. These were not hollow differences. With recognized distinctions like haves *vs.* have-nots, men *vs.* women, high *vs.* the low, aristocrats *vs.* plebeians and with inequalities in authority, a political relationship came into being. However, it must be pointed out that these differences are not the only reason for the formation of an authoritarian structure on the basis of inequalities and disparities.

The social forces that have gained a hegemonic hold have been taking care of these inequities through ideological and violent means to ensure that a social structure based on inequalities is perpetuated. However, there are also movements that have been fighting biased authoritarian structures. Efforts to eliminate oppression of women, private ownership of property and the hold of caste keep emerging in support of an equal social authority. We see that many forces have been fighting inequality and the resultant unjust treatment of people. But there is still some justification for putting forward the case of marginalized people like tribals, women and dalits. To put it briefly, these three categories of people have been ignored by those who have so far fought inequality, bias and injustice. (There are some 'progressives', not from any of the above three categories, who can produce a list of people subjected to even more neglect, as mentioned earlier. These progressives want to prove the point that their concern is much wider than others'.) Tribal people, women and dalits have been ignored both by the hegemonic forces and those opposed to these forces. Those who proceed to study subaltern issues should bear this in mind. In traditional agricultural methods and in modern technological processes, these three categories of subaltern people could not grow to the standards of others in society. Their growth was stifled. Their cultures, civilization and interests were destroyed. No one cared for them nor did anyone take their interests into account.

In Tamil Nadu, for millennia, tribal people have lived by gathering food in hills, arid lands, coastal areas and forests. It is a wonder that even today they are living in the same civilizational state. The voice of these people and those who spoke for them were not heard all these years. Even when it was raised, however meekly, it was neglected or silenced as contrary to the politics of hegemonic forces or as backward. Or their voices were misappropriated for the benefit of varied forces. An example of this is the story of Kannappa Nayanar, the tribal hunter who donated both his eyes as an offering to Lord Siva.

In the history of civilization, women have been used. They were labelled 'Shakthi' and burnt by men. When forests were cleared and converted into agricultural fields, when the harvest of paddy and the land on which it was grown became private property, when kingdoms, wars and temples appeared to defend these properties, the reproductive power and physical labour of women were used for the benefit of patriarchal society. Even after modern industrial production methods appeared and values such as equality and individual freedom and rights gained prominence, feminine powers continue to be used as mere inputs. The forces that fought for economic equality ignored gender equality. They continue to ignore it. The male powers that struggled to bring about equality in other dimensions were not prepared to support gender equality.

In patriarchal society many terms are used to describe women: love, chastity, beauty, flower, power, swan, peacock, cuckoo, mother, devoted wife, and deity and are thus trammelled by golden fetters. On the other hand, women are also despised as liars, as ghosts, as whores, as widows, as barren women, as mayas, as seductresses, as prostitutes, and bound in violent handcuffs. All through history you do not hear the true voice of women. Even if you do, it has been modified to work towards the well-being of menfolk. Some examples from our literature are Madhavi, Manimekalai, Kannagi and Karaikal Ammaiyar. From Andal to the female characters in the novels of Thi. Janakiraman there are many more.

History and politics written from the perception of women is central to subaltern history. Equality and freedom should be reinterpreted from their point of view and that should lead to social transformation. Social transformation should be decided in such a historiography born out of a reinterpretation, and the understanding of women's issues. The Sastras, traditions, philosophies, definitions of morality, theories, forms and protests of others have not delivered justice. We do not need an era of angels. What is needed now is an epoch of women.

The dalits are included in the masses of subaltern people. Before Ranajit Guha examined the culture, protest methods and liberation of these people in the 1960s; Dr. Ambedkar between 1930 and the 1950s; and at the end of the nineteenth century and the beginning of the twentieth century in Tamil Nadu, K. Iyothee Thass Pandithar carried on a struggle on behalf of dalit politics and dalit economic liberation. Towards that goal they strove to eliminate caste and promote Navayana Buddhism. In Tamil Nadu, before Iyothee Thass, Ramalinga Adigal (Vallalar) who came in the intellectual tradition of siddhars declared caste, religion and Sastras irrelevant. The siddhars had raised their voice against religion and caste structure. Even before them, the Sanathanists preached that piety could lead one to heaven, no matter to what caste one belonged. However they pointed out that each caste had its own rules of piety and that these had to be strictly adhered to. For example there was the story of the Saivite saint Nandanar, a dalit farmhand, later known as Thirunalaippovaar (see Essays 4 and 5). Before the Bakthi movement, Buddhist and Jain movements raised their voice against the varna system and the rules related to it.

Dr. Ambedkar

In Tamil Nadu, Iyothee Thass's 'Uplift of Harijans and Elimination of Untouchability' found a place in the agenda of the nationalist movement. Nationalist poet Subramania Bharathi declared that 'there is no such thing as Caste' and also said 'there are a thousand castes here'.[2] The Dravidian Self-Respect movement took up the cause of women and the development of Adi Dravida people. Both in the Right-wing camp and in the Left-wing Communist camp Harijan Uplift Day was observed every year. An unconvincing Marxist clarification was given to dalit problems. They said that when the working class grows powerful, just as with the class system, caste will also wither away and there will be no problems. However, the matter stopped with this explanation and dalits continued to be oppressed and humiliated. In Indian society, you could hear casteist echoes in the heartbeats of people from all classes. Emotionally, the comrades and the darlings of various Dravida Kazhakams live according to their respective caste. Even if intellectually convinced, nobody lets go of caste affiliations. The theory of 'son of the soil' is a cunning device of modern political movements which acts as an extension of the caste scheme.

E. V. Ramaswami Periyar said that only by abolishing Hinduism can we destroy the curse of caste.[3] Though many from his movement left Hinduism, they did not shed their caste loyalty. In subduing dalits and in nursing their own caste loyalty the Kazhagam people were equal to believers. Like capitalism, casteism has acquired an independent existence and is sturdy enough to survive any kind of change.

Jainism, Buddhism, the Bakthi movement, siddhar philosophy, the Communist movement, and conversion to Christianity, secular government, high-placed jobs, education, and modern styles of life and inter-caste marriages, none of these could eradicate caste or end the subordination of women. Schemes for tribal welfare were not concerned with the liberation of these neglected people. So there is pressure now on dalits to bring about social and political changes from their own perspective. From the discussion so far it is clear that tribals, women and dalits need to change the unequal exercise of authority. They have to acquire power for themselves and achieve this from their perspective.

II

Next we have to pay attention to the history of the subaltern, if there is such a history. History depends on who writes it, about whom and for whom. In a society where there is uneven exercise of authority there cannot be a single history. Many histories are possible. Among these, the history of the hegemonic forces is established as the history of the whole society, of the whole nation. In other words, history is written about the manner in which the hegemonic forces established their power through politics. History and politics are not separate entities. They are but two sides of a single coin. All the histories written so far have been scripted by the forces dominating society in various periods of time. They have all been written from the position of authority and have been designed and written by elitist intellectuals.

Taking the Vedas as sacred texts, orthodox groups scripted history in the form of epics, mythology, grammar, and commentaries, Dharmasastras and Upanishads. In this sanctified version of orthodox history, tribal people, women and low-caste people were categorized as pollutants and kept out of the scheme of things. Women were seen as mere bodies meant for human reproduction; tribal people and dalits were identified as bodies helping to produce wealth and food for upper-caste people. The rules created out of the Sastras of orthodox history were implemented in society through the four agencies of mother, father, teacher (guru) and God.

In order to counter the effect of vedic orthodox history, Jainism and Buddhism through their Dharma texts documented an alternative history. This history was that of the warrior and trading communities. According to this history, which expounded the theory of fate, tribal people were looked upon as only half-human and women were declared unfit for enlightenment. It was stated that it was evil deeds such as murder, theft, alcohol, lust and meat-eating that led one to be born a tribal or a woman. These uncared for people were despised as having no control over their senses. In the course of time, with the help of new strategies, vedic orthodoxy, crushed and exiled both Buddhism and Jainism. During the colonial period, in the nineteenth and twentieth centuries, it was believed that European historiography was an intellectual dispassionate work and therefore impartial. European powers that had established colonies in American, African and Asian continents through violent imperialistic methods eulogized their own white culture as superior and derided as primitive the culture of the people they conquered. This eurocentric historiography chronicled the history of Asian-African nations from the same point of view. Indian history was written from European perspectives.

The Indian Nationalist movement against British imperialism formed its history from Hindutva and Indo-European racism. The Hindutva of Indian nationalism wrote Hindu nationalist history with the specific purpose of bulldozing into one rubric numerous nationalities with distinct cultures that had lived on the Indian subcontinent from time immemorial. History was written projecting Rama, Bharatha and Manu as the iconic heroes of Hindu nationalism. Gandhism was a handy support for this ideology. In Hindu nationalist history that glorified traditional ideas of the varnasrama system, the superiority of the Aryans and caste-based vocations, there was no hope of salvation for tribal people, women and dalits. New terms like Girijan, Harijan and Annapurni were given to them but no change was permitted in their lives.

Meanwhile in Tamil Nadu, a new history was being spun with vellalas and Saivism as the epicentre, invoking Agamas, Sastras of Saiva Sidhandha, the hymns of *Thevaram* and *Thiruvasakam*, temples, monasteries and the fervour for Pure Tamil (see also Essays 3 and 4). From the Aryan-Dravidian concept found in Indian history written by Europeans, vellalas identified themselves as Dravidians. The history of Tamils and Dravidians was seen as starting from the period predating 'Sangam' literature. The leadership of Dravidian history, written to counter brahmin domination, passed into the hands of vellalas. In this history, though the honour and bravery of Tamil women was hyped, there was nothing about gender equality. In the history that vellalas wrote, all the non-brahmins were categorized as Dravidian and all the panchamars were identified as Adi Dravidas. The term 'panchamar' was carefully retained among the Tamil castes.

From the Communist movement's viewpoint, in the manner in which they had understood Marxist-Maoist creeds, Indian social history was written on the basis of class. Indian society was defined in terms of semi-feudalism and the nationalist capitalism of the imperialists. Among class differences tribal people and dalits lost their political identity. In reality it was ensured that they never forgot that they were tribal people, women and dalits. By harping on class contradictions as the factor to be eliminated, conflicts arising out of birth or pollution were ignored as being minor. It was pointed out that these problems would disappear after the revolution, when a classless society came into being.

What is clear from the above discussion is that the problems of those who occupy key positions in an authoritarian structure were handled first and it was their story which became history. If they are ever to move closer to power the subaltern masses should write their own history. They should put forward their problems as the main issues and re-write history from their own point of view. In fact they cannot and should not write this history in any other way. In this view, the history they write will be final and facilitate the upliftment of the whole society. (Sounds like a dream!)

III

Finally, there is the Himalayan question that we face of how to bring about social transformation towards equality from the perspective of the subaltern masses. The discussion so far about who these people are and how their history differs from other peoples' has provided some idea about the history of these people and the kind of social change needed.

With the privilege of being upper caste and of being male, that comes gratis with birth, without any effort on their part, upper-caste men are able to exert authority over dalits and women. So they will never advocate caste parity or gender equality. There can be some exceptions to this rule. Leaders like Dr. Ambedkar and E. V. Ramasami Periyar have pleaded that to enjoy the rights and privileges that come as accidents of birth, to exercise control over and to enslave are against human intelligence and dignity. But their voices have been raised in vain. Casteism and patriarchy have not been affected by factors like rationalism, science or atheism. They continue to flourish amidst all the modern, liberal creeds. In spite of all the hurdles in their way, when tribals, women and dalits try to prove themselves through sheer hard work they are derided for their birth. Their basic rights are denied.

Though our society never tires of talking about compassion, grace, love, dharma and kindness, it is in Indian society that a large majority of people are humiliated in the name of gender or caste. Those who indulge in such abuse, support a caste-based, gender-based social structure. They would like this structure to be perpetuated, and they work towards this goal. They convince themselves that it is fate, the result of karma or wages of sin, that one is born tribal, women or dalit.

If we are to abolish the contemptible prejudices relating to differences in birth, in vocations, in physical features, we have to destroy the hegemonic ideology that brought about these constructs. We have to continue the work of demolition that has been started in this matter. All the concepts of the dominant belief system that gave form to these constructs should be re-examined. This would be part of the liberation politics that can expose the absurdities of these constructs. Then their weakness, unfairness and stupidity will also be revealed. The canards of the oppressive, dominant ideology built up by some have been opposed by others from their own side. So the contradictory factors in their belief system should be identified and appropriated. Lastly, the ludicrous traits attributed to birth, and the values attached to them, should be annihilated. For this purpose a powerful, feminist, dalit and tribal discourse should begin on a large scale. And the ideas born out of such a discussion should reach the subconscious through traditional agencies like mother, father, teacher and God. Casteism and patriarchy, embedded in the subconscious, should be peeled off.

There should be a rise in political and intellectual discourse so that there can be a re-examination from the subaltern point of view leading to social change. We should not permit hegemonic political discourses that justify birth-based disparities of gender, caste and race to flourish. They justify the biased exercise of authority over the subaltern. Such beliefs should be exposed and appropriated. This is an important task on the political agenda of Subaltern Studies.

Paper read on 19 September 2006 at the Department of Christian Studies in University of Madras, Chennai.

Notes

1 Julia Kristeva, *Strangers to Ourselves* (New York: Columbia University Press, 1991).

2 Subramania Bharathi, 'Bharathiyaar Kavithaikal', song titled 'Vandematharam' (Chennai: Kaliswari Pathipakam, 2012).

3 Periyar E. V. R. *Chindhanaigal* (Thoughts of EVR), V.Anaimuthu, ed. (Tirchi: Thinkers Forum, 1974): 1391.

8

Religion (Hinduism) from the Dalit Perspective

I WOULD LIKE to clarify at the start that in this essay we are concerned about dalits and religion, so we will move away from the common view of religion and discuss it only from the dalit perspective. In India we have a caste group referred to as dalits, a product of Hindu religious culture, not found anywhere else in the world. So in this essay we will be concerned specifically about Hinduism, from which a caste-based society originated, and not about religion in general. One has to look at Hinduism through the eyes of dalits because it is they who have been adversely impacted by it. In fact, one has to look at the antitheses of Hinduism, the reform movements, the renewal efforts since the time before Christ (in the Indian subcontinent), beginning with Buddhism, Jainism then after Sikhism, the siddhar ideology, different kinds of other creeds, like Islam and Christianity from the West. All these belief systems were absorbed by the varna-caste structure of Hinduism. We will have to look at this accommodation of the caste system by different ideologies from the dalit perspective. But that would be far beyond the brief of this essay and so it has not been attempted.

Hinduism and related faiths have directly or indirectly created the stigma attributed to the working classes concerning impurity on the basis of birth. Consequently these people are oppressed, marginalized and rendered unequal to others.

150

So you cannot expect an examination of Hinduism to be objective as per research rituals/traditions. In a non-egalitarian society like ours, even a credo like objectivity can turn out to be an instrument of ideological oppression.

I

In this essay I have not taken into consideration the theology of a religion, its spiritual doctrine, and spiritual uplift, discussions glorifying God, social cohesion and civilizational growth. That kind of a discussion is not the immediate need of a dalit. What is the point in discussing these concepts which did not help in redeeming him or her from the ignominy attributed to his or her birth? From the point of view of a dalit, these ideas are to be discussed and mulled over by those considered of superior birth.

During the nineteenth and the first half of the twentieth centuries, British rule enabled the dalit forerunners Iyothee Thass (1845–1914) and Dr. Ambedkar (1891–1956) to grow acquainted with modern ideas (see Essay 7). It is necessary to first understand how they approached Hinduism during their active years. Along with that, we should add views of E. V. Ramasami Periyar (1879–1973) on the welfare of the shudras, which was based on his atheistic doctrine (see Essay 7). These three leaders provided the base for the dalit perspective on religion. During the period in which they lived, momentous changes were taking place rapidly. On the plane of politics, economics, culture and civilization there were unprecedented historical changes, growth and obliterations. This period was also a time when people immersed in a traditional pattern of life, formed caste forums, caste groups and class-based formations to guard their interests and involved themselves in many struggles and competitions. Iyothee Thass and Dr. Ambedkar slogged for the welfare of dalits and for the eradication of untouchability while Periyar worked for social justice and the self-esteem of shudras.

Iyothee Thass

A dalit from the Nilgiris, he was one of the significant dalit intellectuals who accessed modern education, employment, culture, and material comforts through opportunities created by British rule (see also Chapter 9). He was a many-sided personality: a journalist, a Siddha doctor, a Tamil pundit and a polyglot. He started a discourse for the marginalized even before Dr. Ambedkar and Periyar did. He held that the dalits of India, who form one-sixth of the population of the country, were the ancient, casteless, Dravidian Buddhists. He wrote a social history that the brahmins, through their chicanery, through the caste-bound Hindu religion, marginalized and relegated this working class of one-sixth to be untouchables.

Iyothee Thass explained his understanding of the correlation between caste divisions and Hinduism. 'Caste divisions are the basis of Hinduism; Hinduism is the basis of caste divisions'.[1] He was clear that economic considerations are the fundamental reasons for caste gradations. In 1907 he wrote in his magazine *Thamizhan* that the lower castes should reject the stories spun by the upper castes for their livelihood.[2] He raised his voice against the blocs that opposed the progress of dalits in the name of religion and caste. The dalits who had thus remained neglected were beginning to enjoy the benefits of the new economic system during the British period. He questioned the wisdom of dalit conversion to Christianity and Islam in order to take the path of development, while the caste Hindus could achieve this without conversion. Thass knew well that these new opportunities were beneficial for the people from the privileged caste groups who had facilitated the formation of Hindu society.

He pointed out how by clever planning dalits were distanced on the basis of caste and the Sastras from all useful, favourable, clean, hygienic, economically advantageous situations.[3] For example, in the early years, upper-caste people, on the basis of caste and religious orthodoxy, refused to enlist in the army, the medical field, and the educational institutions founded by the missionaries. They also refused to engage with Christianity; while others considered these fields as militating against their tenets, the dalits, untrammelled as they were by orthodoxy, associated themselves with these and benefited. They tasted the benefits of 'modern life'. Modernity was in conflict with Hinduism and its canons. Thass laments that the upper-caste Hindus on observing the progress made by the dalits, decided to enter these fields themselves. Ignoring the canons of the Sastras they embraced Christianity and pushed the dalits out of these fields by citing the good old caste customs.[4] The higher castes, sticking to the orthodox rules of caste and religion, have propagated the tricks related to these two factors. They paid no attention to the toil related to agriculture, to the modern instruments connected with it like irrigation, equipment, de-husking implements or to the new discoveries of science like photography, telegraphy, railways or tramways.[5] Yet, they could easily appropriate the benefits of these new discoveries because of the dominant position they held in the old order of caste-religion. Thass pointed out how even the Indian National Congress acted as if it were 'Hindu National Congress or Brahmin National Congress'.[6] Even outfits like The Madras Industrial Association, when it collected funds for public matters, did not go by caste considerations but while spending it, dalits were ignored.[7] What Thass observed about the functioning of the Benares Hindu University was enough to explain the caste basis of Hinduism.

> Even as the term 'Hindu' appeared it was evident that caste and religious discriminations were to be the inference of direct perception.[8]

It is clear from the above that if one does not believe in caste divisions one cannot be a Hindu. Thass pointed out that these divisions have affected agriculture adversely. Due to the caste structure, farming got degraded, paving the way for famine.[9] British rule, taxation, its exploitative methods, low rainfall and drought are conventionally pointed out as the causes for famine. However, more than all these factors, it was the labelling of the agricultural labourers as untouchables that was the reason. They were alienated from the land and were made into a mass of hungry people. Consequently, in the Tamil country for a long time there has been hunger, poverty, begging and alms giving as part of day-to-day life. The methods to counter this situation such as philanthropy, medical aid, feeding of the poor, charities, donations and handouts were hailed as the high ethics of the upper caste. It was Thass who first pointed out the connection between persistent famine and the caste structure of Hinduism.

Ambedkar pointed out that in casteist Hindu society the gradation of lower and higher human beings is more important than the distinction between a good Hindu and a bad Hindu. Attracted by Christianity which preached equality and did not differentiate between people, a large number of dalits converted. However by the efflux of time the upper-caste Hindus changed Christianity also into a caste-based religion by conversion. Observing this, Thass concluded that Christianity will not provide equality to dalits. He did not approve of dalit worship of folk deities. He identified Buddhism as their religion. The dharma that Buddha commended included egalitarianism, equality, ahimsa, justice and compassion. Iyothee Thass was the first dalit ideologue to project the Buddhist Dharma as the creed of dalits.

Let us first look at how Thass viewed Christianity which was looked upon in those days as the alternative religion. Both the Protestant and Roman Catholic Christians had internalized caste divisions like Hinduism, Thass rejected these two. He saw the missionaries as the cause for this development. The dalits who were converted to Roman Catholic Christianity had to live with the same caste identities. Thass pointed out that in addition, they had to pay the padre sizable amounts for the seven sacraments and related services: baptism, confirmation, confession, weekly offertory, marriage, priesthood and the last ceremony.[10] The dalits who joined the Protestant Church, got educated and managed to reach good positions. But some upper-caste Hindus converted and pushed the dalits out from these positions. They referred to atrocities. In fact, Thass pointed out that Christ and his disciples did not collect wealth like the Roman Catholic priests.[11] Thass was aware that caste has no place in Christianity. But in the Indian situation, in day-to-day life, there are people who remain a Hindu from the caste angle but practise Christianity religiously; accepting Brahminism and Christ at the same time. They are half-Christian and half-Hindu.[12] They are Hindu-Christians.

Thass thought that whatever is associated with the caste system and Hinduism cannot be common to all humanity. According to this criterion, Christianity in India had lost its quality of being a universal religion. Similarly the Hindi language, because of its close association with Hinduism, is unfit to be the common language of India. Thass wrote to Periyar that only English was suited for that purpose.[13] Later Periyar said that our language itself safeguards the caste system. He even went to the extent of saying we should make English our mother tongue because it lacks the vocabulary of caste. However, we should not weigh this statement against the political background of today.

Hinduism institutionalized caste. Thass held that Hinduism has been created by some for selfish reasons, to eke out a livelihood and that its purpose is not the elevation of humanity. He wrote 'Toddy shop is a *felony* that *distorts* the senses; *God shop* is a *felony* that *mulcts* people of money.'[14] He said instead of boycotting foreign textiles, we should boycott caste and religion like we would boycott arrack and toddy shops.[15] 'We should collect the stones called caste and the weeds called religion, cast them into the sea and live in harmony with our brothers.'[16] In a similar tone, Ramalinga Adigalar also exhorted people to discard these matters.

Thass rejected caste-ridden Christianity and also the traditional modes of worship of the dalits. The worship of folk deities, that comes with rituals like animal sacrifice was against the principles of Buddhist Dharma in which Thass believed. In April 1892 he was invited to speak on the topic 'The Pariah Problem' in the Chennai Mahajana Sabha. He talked about the equal rights of all castes to enter Hindu temples. A person called Sivarama Sastri who responded to Thass said, 'We have given for your community gods like Maduraiveeran, Kaateri, and Karuppannan. Sivan and Vishnu are not meant for your community.'[17] Though Sivarama Sastri's talk might appear strange to present-day liberals; the truth is that caste discrimination has persisted in some form or the other secretly.

Replying to Sastri, Thass said, 'We do not want your gods: the Pariah children should be provided with schools in each village, with free education up to fourth standard. Land should be given to the people in the Pariah villages.'[18]

Finally as an alternative religion for the dalits, Thass pointed to Buddhism as

> Respect for all life forms and compassionate acts
> *are the essence of Buddha Dharma.* (vol. 2:118)

The Dharma of Buddhism had included principles such as love, sympathy, intelligence, equality, justice and discipline and could be the path for an educated gentleman. For the dalits, who are unable to reach these values, it can only be an ideal. Thass saw Buddhism as an alternative religion to Saivism which was prevalent during his times.

Dr. Babasaheb Ambedkar

Though he is described as a pioneer Marathi dalit intellectual who wrote and fought for oppressed dalits across the country, he is much more than that: one of the geniuses of modern India. Dr. Ambedkar excelled in Western education and also in the traditional Indian method of learning: He was familiar with the liberal thought of the British tradition.

Dr. Ambedkar firmly believed that 'for human life religion is essential'. But in India 'what is known as religion is not religion at all. Only a set of rules'.[19] He differentiated his ideal religion from the Hinduism that existed. His ideal consisted of modern democratic principles that included freedom, equality and brotherhood. He did not plan to destroy Hinduism but he said that Brahminism should be eradicated and Hinduism saved.[20] Eradicating Brahminism meant doing away with the caste system and caste discrimination. For this we have to remove the dominance of the Vedas and Sastras. Like Buddha and Guru Nanak, we have to deny the authority of the Sastras.[21] Of course Hinduism will try to prevent this. So Ambedkar's early thoughts were to extract the essence of the Upanishads, by jettisoning some portions, inserting some new concepts and bringing about an innovative religion.[22] Influenced by the thinkers of his time, Ambedkar thought he could extract the exceptional features from ancient culture, adapt them to modernity and forge a new path.

Dr. Ambedkar respected religion and believed that it could activate one's conscience and direct it towards social justice.[23] On the other hand, through rationalism (read atheism) it is difficult to bring about social justice. He wrote about the limitations of atheism and rationalism. As long as it does not come into conflict with caste and class loyalties of the rationalist who professes atheistic ideas, his rationalism will work. If it touches the rationalist's interests, then it would fail.[24] Similarly, religion too can deliver justice only within one race, clan or caste. Religion cannot deliver when these different identities are at work. He pointed out as an example the case of whites and blacks in America where Christianity could not bring about equal justice. Therefore, in India we can never expect Hinduism to bring about social justice for the untouchables. The reason is that for the Hindu his caste is sacred, and permanent; it is his religious foundation which makes him believe in this.[25] A Hindu believes that God created caste. Dr. Ambedkar thought this was unfortunate.

The basic unit of the caste discrimination of Hinduism is untouchability and Ambedkar's ideas on this subject are important. All over the world from ancient puranic times people believed that by touching some objects or people, filth, dirt or pollutant can be contacted and spread. Similarly some believed that evil could be spread. They held that this kind of contamination could happen through eating and drinking as if it were contagious. On the same lines they believed that birth, puberty, wedding, copulation and death can also cause pollution. Individuals polluted by these factors were quarantined for some time. The mother in childbirth, the woman after puberty and during menstruation, men and women during marriage or inappropriate acts of sex; in death the corpse and its relatives were isolated. Water and blood functioned as the purifying elements. (In vedic religion fire had an important role.) Such practices prevailed all over the world but there is an important difference between Hindus and the rest. In Hindu culture, not a few individuals, but certain sections of people are treated as untouchables and polluted on the basis of birth and were segregated permanently. Nowhere else in the world can this practice be found. What was temporarily imposed in the Hindu tradition was made lasting on a group of people on the basis of their birth.[26] (It is because of this feature, that dalit liberation is not possible by an individual but only by all the mass of dalit people, see Essay 5.)

There was another dimension to this pollution aspect. If this mass of people, declared perpetually polluted on the basis of birth, touch any sacred place or artifact and individuals, then all are affected by pollution. The penalty of untouchability was slapped on the mass of people who lost in the struggle for supremacy between the brahmins and Buddhists that lasted from AD 400 to AD 600.[27] Iyothee Thass has expressed the same thought. There is a historical basis in the plea of both these thinkers that to liberate themselves from untouchability dalits must change to Buddha Dharma.

It was not Ambedkar's idea to remove religion from human life. He tried to find the origin of religion in the doctrines of tribal society, their symbols and what they shunned. The original belief of tribal society was oriented towards nurturing the lifestyle of the people. At the ideological level, it tried to counterbalance the total inability of human groups against the might of nature. Dr. Ambedkar points out that when tribal society disappeared giving place to a new civilization, God took the place of this old ideology. Thus from the beginning religion was not concerned about individuals but with society.[28] Like language, religion also made individual human beings relate to society. In this, religion functioned as a mechanism to regulate society.[29] There is no doubt that all these ideas of Ambedkar were a result of his Western education. If we examine this concept we observe that at all times to compensate for its sense of helplessness, human society follows in one form or the other the old magic and totems of the tribes. Atheism, which ridicules theism, can function as a substitute for religion for some people. Similarly intellect and science can fulfil the role of religion. This of course needs deeper enquiry.

Though intellectually Ambedkar appreciated the need for and the role of religion, he did not approve of Hinduism which had created caste for social control on the basis of discrimination. He declared, 'O Hinduism! Thy name is inequality' and 'The very soul of Hinduism is inequality'.[30] That kind of a Hinduism is a religion that stops with temples; there is no place in it for love. Therefore, he said, it cannot love fellow human beings or render any service to them. Though religion, like language can facilitate social relations, here it seems to function with prejudice. He said that the thought of service and of freedom, equality and brotherhood are alien to Hinduism because it rests on caste discrimination.[31] Every Hindu thinks about another person only in terms of higher or lower and never in terms of being equal. His conclusion was,

> For Hindus inequality is a lifestyle ordained by God; it's a
> religious doctrine; lifestyle. To this extent it is an ineradi-
> cable feature of Hinduism. The concept of inequality has
> been built into the thought and action of Hindu Society
> (Ibid: vol.4:66).

This idea can even be taken as the dalit view of religion.
Ambedkar made a number of insightful observations about
brahminic Hindu social structure. He pointed out how it
had been laid down that Hindu social organization has been
created by God; it is based on a hierarchical gradation; Caste-
based vocation was decided by birth: there should be no
intermingling of caste; in this scheme of things the brahmins
are the preeminent humans; Everything has been formed
with their well-being in mind; towards this end, the socio-
economic standard of the oppressed caste people was kept at
a low level by means of ignorance and violence.[32]

All societies in the world have class distinctions. They
are normal and natural. However, these natural differences
were not glorified as an everlasting ideal. Ambedkar pointed
out that in the brahminic Vedas, the portion titled 'Purusha
Suktham' extolled these class differences as being the ideal,
sacred and divine and he refuted that stand. He said that brahmins guarded and nurtured Hinduism because the structure
of graded society helped in maintaining their hegemonic hold
over people.[33]

E. V. Ramasami Periyar

When the dalit thinkers of the nineteenth and twentieth
centuries like Iyothee Thass and Ambedkar put forward ideas
about Hinduism, based on their own experience and on the
basis of history, the argument for eradication of caste was
stronger than that which called for the abolition of religion.
They saw the need for a religious order based on equality
and on the rights of individual human beings. Buddhism was
the obvious answer.

Periyar was a contemporary of these thinkers and was active even after them. Unlike Navayana Guru, he believed that abolition of Hinduism along with God, Sastras and Puranas was a prerequisite for the eradication of caste. Without compromising on this stand, he organized agitations one after the other. Periyar, who saw himself as a shudra, considered liberation of the shudras to be of prime importance. He believed that brahminic Hinduism referred to the shudras as the children of prostitutes; it marginalized the Panchamar castes as untouchables. Women were enslaved by their very birth. Therefore, Periyar's basic stand was that all those affected by Brahminism should be liberated.

'There is no other way but to confront and destroy religion (the basis for caste) and the God who is supposed to have created that religion' said Periyar. [34] He stated that generally religion ruins intellect; facilitates divisions; encourages hypocrisy; displacing reasoning, it creates touts between God and people. It makes cowards of people. It makes some live on the toil of others. [35] One can observe how Periyar differs from Dr. Ambedkar.

Periyar said that where there is religion, there intellect and equality are not respected. He held that intellect and equality are related to atheism and rationalism. [36] According to him, social equality and economic equality are brought about by the rationalism of atheism and self-respect. God and religion are diametrically opposed to these two kinds of equality. In the Indian context, for economic (class) disparities, caste is the reason; Periyar's thesis was that the Hindu religion was the reason for caste differences. Hard work is not enough to attain economic status. What is required is appropriate caste right. Religion causes caste variations which in turn creates economic dissimilarities. It guards these differences. Periyar cautioned that even after socialist oriented changes have come about, caste divisions have taken things back to former conditions. In other words, social disparities based on birth will continue to operate even where one is trying to bring about economic equality.[37] To bring about economic equality, caste differences have to be abolished. To remove caste divisions, Hinduism and related religions should be wiped out. To move towards this goal, ideas of self-respect and rationalism should be disseminated widely.

There is no doubt that the action plan and ideology of Periyar are radical: To demolish Hinduism and related beliefs, an awareness and knowledge of self-respect, rationalism, egalitarianism and atheism are basic requirements. So the situation now is contrary. Considerable numbers of Indians, who became atheists and rationalists, now are busy protecting their caste interests and in the name of their caste are aiming to capture governmental power, social power and economic power. In this matter there is no difference between them and the theists who are staunch Hindus. Actually without giving up caste and caste loyalties one can function as an atheist and a rationalist. Every Hindu born in Indian culture nurtures caste feeling.[38] In this context we have to bear in mind the statement of Ambedkar: 'No other loyalty can prevent a Hindu from the duty of defending his caste.' Whether he converts to Christianity or rejects religion and becomes an atheist, a Hindu's loyalty to caste does not change. Therefore the concept of annihilation of caste advocated by Iyothee Thass and Ambedkar has become more important than the eradication of religion advocated by Periyar. However, compared to abolition of religion, obliteration of caste is not so easy. This is because for doing away with religion the basis is intellectual thinking; but to get rid of caste one has to work at the subconscious level. Changing one's feelings is more difficult than changing one's ideas and thinking. Though Ambedkar included in his caste eradication plan, inter-caste marriage, rejection of Sastras and their authority over people, at one stage he wrote that it is virtually impossible to demolish the caste system among the Hindus. There is good reason for the stand he took. Since everyone is a slave to this caste system, status and human rights have been unequally distributed according one's caste, Ambedkar wrote that it is next to impossible to break the caste structure.[39]

Periyar held that God and religion (Hinduism) protect caste and class differences. Moreover, government, literature and language are also performing this function. In the government of Hindus, their literature and language casteism pervade directly or in the form of symbols. This is the reason Periyar described religion as a disease.[40] Iyothee Thass and Ambedkar would have seen caste as a disease rather than religion.

Therefore, it is clear that even if a Hindu eschews religion and God, he/she can continue to live as an individual of a specific caste. It can be observed that the agitations led by Thass, Ambedkar and Periyar at different times to eradicate caste and religion were in practice and in principle, struggles on behalf of dalits. As far as shudras are concerned, such protests could be ploys for their own empowerment and advancement. Self-respect and egalitarianism (socialism), the factors Periyar spoke about, can be operative within each caste but not among different castes, particularly not between dalits and non-dalits. This is the practical truth. In principle, dalits have nothing to lose by the eradication of religion and caste. But others, particularly the shudras, may lose their caste status. This is the reasons for the frequent violence against dalits.

The writings of Iyothee Thass and Ambedkar about religion form the basis of the dalit viewpoint on the subject. These are the early expressions of awareness on the part of educated dalits during British rule, and were a result of the impact of modernity. These two thinkers clearly delineated the direct connection between brahminic Hinduism and the formation of a society with caste and class differences. Both firmly believed the history of how dalits came to be oppressed and marginalized by Brahminism on the basis of untouchability. As an alternative to brahminic religion they both felt the need for a new religion that would embrace the whole human race, with equality, good conduct, justice, love and compassion. They concluded that the caste system and untouchability have been deployed only to facilitate the dominance, prosperity, enjoyment and welfare of brahmins and the Hindus who believe in caste differences. The two discerned that caste structure and untouchability go against human dignity, honour and ethics. Thass perceived compassion, generosity, science and brotherhood could be the ideological basis for a new society. For Dr. Ambedkar freedom, equality, brotherhood, individual liberty within democracy, hard work, skill and education were the basis for that same order. Periyar, on the other hand, internalized these modern ideas through his concepts of atheism, rationalism, self-respect and egalitarianism. He put forward an honourable religion based on intellect in the place of Hinduism. He said that in the age of electricity Hinduism was inappropriate. Instead of the archaic Sanathana religion with discriminations and superstitions as its basic principles, we should have new disciplines and values. These should be without affecting individual freedom, without graded differences, in harmony with nature and acceptable to our intelligence, possibilities and experience. Explaining his Self-Respect movement he said that meaningless practices, superstitions and empty rituals and the expenses incurred for them should be done away with. The disparities created in the name of caste, religion and class, the inequalities in the social and economic sectors should be removed and everyone should live as one society in brotherhood. We should create a feeling of self-respect among people so that they would live by reason and self-respect.[41] One can discern the basics of his religion of intellect in the above objectives. Periyar said that the duty of a rational human being is to have love, concern for all life forms, intellect and truth as the basis and remove all that is opposed to these principles.[42] This stand of Periyar in fact reveals his involvement with tradition. These ideas can be clearly recognized in the continuum of Buddhism, Jainism, siddhars and the ideas of Ramalingar.

Today, religion has been utterly commercialized and politics has become a weapon in the struggle between majority against minority. On the one hand, religion has laid the foundation for fundamentalism and, on the other hand, for extremism. At the national and international level it has become a problem. Fascism has raised its head in the name of religion. Against this background, in India, different castes and caste formations are trying to get power through representative politics so that each might raise his own caste to a better position. They are not at all interested in eradicating caste. Caste loyalties pervade democratic politics.

Against this backdrop, the relationship between a dalit and religion is unclear. Since the idea of dalit liberation has become multifaceted among dalit groups, there is no consensus on the religion of dalits. In the rural areas, folk religion involving worship of folk deity and clan deity is still popular. The position is the same among the backward classes with similar lifestyles as the dalits. Among the dalits, folk deity worship expresses itself in votive offerings, pongal, and other such rites. These function as symbols of collective dalit strength, their community bond, security and prestige. After the educated dalits migrated to cities, they either become Sanskritized or get converted to Christianity and attach themselves to different religions and live as progressive people.

Whichever way we look at it, it is clear that the hold of primordial religion is still strong among dalits. The need for a religion is constantly felt by them, either for existential reasons, for comfort or to escape caste-related indignities. The feeling for the old religion of magic, totemic symbols is embedded in them. Because of the pressures of life, they have to find support for their existence, their attachments within themselves, within their communal life. They need their religion to protect themselves, and their community from poverty, privation, ignorance, fear and untouchability. Atheism could not have defended them. The new religion that Iyothee Thass and Ambedkar advocated is an ideal for the whole human race. It cannot contribute anything today

to the existential problems of dalits. A society sans caste and
religion differences may be an attractive concept but is not
pragmatic. Only their folk deities and family gods can provide
the psychological strength required to carry on the struggle
of the dalits to eradicate the caste system. It is a dead end!

Presented at Guru Nanak Peedam, Madurai Kamarasar University, on
17 August 2002. Published in *Dalitiya Vimarisana Katturaikal* (Nagercoil:
Kalachuvadu, 2003).

Notes

1 Ka. Iyothee Thass, *Chintanaigal. Nattar Valakkatriyal Aayvu Maiyam,*
   vol 2 (1999): 181.
2 Ibid.: 34.
3 Ibid.: 3–8.
4 Ibid.: 65–66.
5 Ibid.:72.
6 Ibid.: 77.
7 Ibid.:79
8 Ibid: 335 (1911).
9 Ibid.: 197.
10 Ibid.: .88–89.
11 Ibid.: 90–91.
12 Ibid.: 688 (1910).
13 Ibid.: 326 (1911).
14 Ibid.: 211 (1909).
15 Ibid.: 36..
16 Ibid.: 28 (1907).
17 Ibid. 80.
18 Ibid.:80–81 (1908).
19 B. R. Ambedkar and Vasant Moon, 1979. *Dr. Babasaheb Ambedkar:Writings
   and Speeches.*, 22 vols. (Bombay: Government of Maharashtra, Department
   of Education., 1979–2010): vol. 2: 91; vol. 1: 90.
20 Ibid.: vol. 2: 93.
21 Ibid.: vol.1: 87; vol.2 :74.
22 Ibid.: vol.2: 94.
23 Ibid.: vol. 5: 396.
24 Ibid.: vol. 5: 397.
25 Ibid.: vo.l 5: 368; vol. 5: 102.
26 Ibid.: vol.7.: 259, 265, 266.

27 Ibid.: vol 7.: 379.
28 Ibid.: vol 5.: 408–09.
29 Ibid.: vol. 5: 410.
30 Ibid.: vol. 4: 87; vol. 3: 66.
31 Ibid.: vol. 5.: 451.
32 Ibid.: vol. 4: 126.
33 Ibid.: vol. 7: 240; 726.
34 V. Anaimuthu, *Periyar E. Ve. Ra.. Chintanaikal,* 3 vols. (Tiruchi: Patipp-
    aciriyar Munnurai, Chintanaiyalar Kalakam, 1974: vol. 1: 57–58.
35 Ibid.: vol. 2: 1055, 1949.
36 Ibid.: vol.2: 1108.
37 Ibid.: vol. 3: 1691, 1700, 1704.
38 Ibid.: vol.2.: 32.
39 Ibid.: vol 2.: 81–82, 87.
40 Ibid.: vol.3: 1627, 1628.
41 Ibid.: vol. 2: 458, 792.
42 Ibid.: vol.2: 472.

9

The Times of
Iyothee Thass (1845–1914)

THE PERIOD IN which Iyothee Thass lived was a momentous one in the history of India. A society that had been complacent with its archaic production methods and religious hegemony for two thousand years was in the throes of change. The entry of foreigners had brought in cataclysmic changes in people's lives. Though the brahminical forces tried their best to prevent the effects of these changes, the benefits of the new dispensation were enjoyed exclusively by them.'

In fact, this period can be described as one in which upper-caste people acquired Western education and through the power thus gained, organized for themselves a comfortable new life. British imperialism and Brahminism worked jointly to safeguard their respective interests.

Nationalist endeavours that began with submitting petitions to the government, gradually took the form of struggle for independence in the Bengal and Bombay Presidencies, and Punjab. Western types of schools and colleges, religious and educational services offered by Christian missionaries, the response by Nationalists and the newly emerging salaried class had all become novel social realities. Out of the factories and other centres of production, new categories of working classes and capitalists were emerging. Even as they materialized, there were labour actions in the form of strikes in Nagpur (1877) and in Bombay and Madras Presidencies (1882–1890).

Brahminical forces were active in Hinduizing the administration, in infusing extremism into Nationalist agitations, in streamlining rituals and in obtaining government posts. In all centres of power in South India brahmins took up strategic positions. Though their demands were put forward ostensibly with the nation in mind, they were in effect aimed at protecting the economic and social interests of the upper castes. It became apparent that the nationalist movement of those opposing British rule was in fact a movement to revive Hinduism. In the newly appearing political plane, the old intellectuals and administrators receded to the background and popular political leaders came to the forefront. The Indian National Congress, founded by a few upper-caste and upper-class people moved towards a radical position triggered by the partition of Bengal in 1905. In Bengal a faction of it even took on the characteristics of an underground terrorist movement led by upper-caste youngsters. The moderate faction of the Congress that advocated petitioning and the extremist faction that demanded Independence from British rule, clashed in the Surat Congress. Gandhi, after experimenting with Satyagraha in South Africa, arrived in India in 1914. That was the year Iyothee Thass died.

Historian R. Sundaralingam describes the period in which Iyothee Thass was active as the era of graduate societies.[1] In the latter half of the nineteenth century, in every town in the areas where Western-educated people lived, there was a literary or debating society. He records that in 1886 there were at least 100 such societies in Chennai. In later years many South Indian political leaders were schooled in these societies in which landlords, interpreters, lawyers and graduates were members. The bulk of them were Brahmins. Not only in these societies, but also in the field of journalism, in education, in the legal professions, education and administration brahmins occupied key places. Ever since the administration came into the hands of the British, the bureaucrats and senior executives ran the show. The power of the priesthood in the religious, social and cultural plane, the power of the landlords in the rural agricultural arena, and the power of civil servants in the government in South India were all concentrated in the hands of brahmins.

The world of journalism which controlled the spread of ideas among the Tamil people was also in the hands of brahmin intellectuals. Journalists such as G. Subramaniya Iyer, Kasthurirangan and poet Bharathi were active in this period. The first Tamil daily *Swadesamithran,* founded in 1882, which lasted till 1985, was quite open about safeguarding the interests of brahmins.

At this time, European missionaries founded various societies to propagate the gospel. Following them, some Indian intellectuals started societies and took a series of steps to reform Hinduism. Their aim was to infuse modern values into Hinduism, to reduce the differences among castes, to promote inter-caste marriages, to educate women, to care for the interests of widows, and to eradicate superstitions. But after the partition of Bengal, the reformist agenda took a backseat and political agitations came to the fore. The belief that any talk of social reformation is possible only with complete independence gained currency.

Of the 'societies' engaged in socio-religious reforms, the Theosophical Society had a special place. This society also played a role in the life of Iyothee Thass. In 1882, the society was shifted from Bombay to Adyar in Madras. By 1883, it had at least nine branches in South India. The society got support from upper-caste Hindus, both brahmins and non-brahmins. Hindu government officers who kept aloof from political activities backed this society. In the committees of the branches of this society, local sub-collectors, district munsifs and tahsildars found a place. Lawyers, teachers, journalists and local political leaders were members. The business community funded the society. The first president of the Society, Col. H. S. Olcott, described the supporters as 'The Flower of the Indian people'. Sundaralingam points out that this society earned educated Indians and their nation a sense of self-respect.

But what Sundaralingam failed to mention is that this same society also helped Neo-Buddhists and dalit Buddhists to gain some self-respect. It educated dalit children and backed the efforts of Iyothee Thass and P. Lakshmi Narasu who aimed at social reforms. It supported Neo-Buddhism which engaged itself in social reforms. However, leaders like the poet Bharathi did not approve of the society. So long as Olcott was the president, brahmins did not approve of the society. Only after his death, in 1907, when the society came into the hands of Annie Besant, did it get the support of brahmins.

Convinced of the creed of Buddhism after studying it for a long time, in 1890 Iyothee Thass accepted Buddhism. In 1896 he approached Olcott and sought his support to build a Buddha Vihara and to found a Buddhist Sanga. In 1898, along with Olcott and a friend P. Krishnaswamy, he travelled to Ceylon (now Sri Lanka) and the three were converted to Buddhism at Malikanta Vihara after receiving Panchasheel from Sumangala Mahanayaka. On his return Iyothee Thass, along with his Buddhist friends, in 1898 founded The South Indian Sakya Buddhist Sanga in Royapettai, Chennai. Dr Paul Carus, a philosopher and author of *The Gospel of Buddha*, who was living in Chicago, agreed to be the president. Soon branches came up in Bangalore, Kolar Gold Fields, Tirupathur (near Jolarpettai), Secundarabad, and Rangoon (now known as Yangon). The name of the institution was changed to The South Indian Buddhist Sanga. From 1898 to 1908 this Sanga became the centre of activities related to Buddhism, particularly among dalits. The monthly rent for the building in which the Sanga functioned, ₹10, was paid by Annie Besant. She also gave occasional donations. Buddhists from Kolar Gold Fields collected money and bought a printing machine for the magazine. When Olcott died that year, Iyothee Thass conducted his funeral as requested by Annie Besant according to Buddhist rites.

When he founded the Buddhist Sanga, Iyothee Thass listed its aims as to create a casteless society, gain dignity for dalits, eschew meat and liquor, receive Panchasheel and work towards equality among people. But even as this Sanga was working to eradicate caste, in the branch of the Mahabodhi Sanga started by the Sri Lankan Buddhist revivalist Angarika Dharmapala, located in Pudupettai in Chennai, caste differences were practised. The passion that dalit Buddhists like Iyothee Thass had for removing caste disparities was absent among other Buddhists. To propagate Buddhist Dharma, Iyothee Thass in 1907 started a weekly titled *Thamizhan.*

Researchers G. Aloysius and K. Perumal have brought to light the path-breaking work done by Iyothee Thass and his friends during the early years of the twentieth century, by working for education and related social uplift in Chennai, Perambur, and Kolar Gold Fields.[2] His supporters idolised him for his work in this field and added a number of honorifics to his name whenever they referred to him. In the face of stiff opposition from brahminic forces, through his magazine and the Sanga, he put forward Buddha Dharma as the religion of Dravidians (read dalits), as the alternative to brahminic Hinduism. Half a century before Ambedkar started the Navayana Buddhist movement, Iyothee Thass had started this work. He could be called the forerunner of Navayana Buddhism. By reinterpreting ancient Tamil literature, *Nigandu,* Buddhist works, ballads and proverbs, Iyothee Thass tried to put forward Buddhism as the original religion of the 'pariahs', of the subalterns. This is his unique contribution. This distinctive feature is revealed in his works *Indhirar Thesa Charithiram* and *Adhi Vedham.*

In the context of the Census, Iyothee Thass made the point that Buddhists, Saivites and Vaishnavites are different from each other. In the 1881 Census, some brahmin officers had suggested that those who are not Christians, Muslims or Sikhs should be counted as Hindus. The British government accepted this suggestion. But Iyothee Thass asked the

authorities to declare Dravidian Buddhists to be Adhi Tamil
(The original Tamils). He kept reiterating this point until it
was accepted in 1911. In the Census of 1921, the number of
Dravidian Buddhists went up considerably.

For these activities Iyothee Thass was targeted by upper-
caste Saivites and Vaishnavites. Rumour was set about that
Nayanmars, Alwars and Jesus were maligned in the Sakya Sanga
and in the Mahabodhi Sanga branch. Well-known thinker
and writer, Thiru. Vi. Kalyanasundaranar and his supporters
created a ruckus during a meeting of the Buddhist Sanga in
Royapettai. K. Vadivelu Chettiar and Vidwan Chennakesavalu
caused a disruption in the proceedings. However, later Thiru.
Vi. Ka changed his stand after studying the Buddhist writings of Olcott, Jinaraja Dasa and Dharmapala. After he was
convinced of the teachings of Buddha, he lectured on topics
such as Buddha Dharma Sanga and went on the write a book
titled *Buddhism in Tamil Literature*. He refers to this work in
his autobiography and also records how Iyothee Thass cured
him of a chronic condition in his leg from which he had suf-
fered for two years when he was a boy. He praises his medical
competence. When Iyothee Thass died Thiru. Vi. Ka wrote a
poem as an obituary.

In 1917 a Buddhist conference which could not be held
in the life time of Iyothee Thass, was held in Madras. It was
the first conference of Buddhists in the Presidency. A reso-
lution to send a petition to the Montague-Chelmsford group
seeking representation for Adi Dravidas was passed at this
conference. In that conference, presided over by P. Lakshmi
Narasu, there were delegates from Colombo, Rangoon,
Mysore and Secunderabad. Following this model, successive
conferences were held in different cities in 1920, 1932 and
1952.

During the time of Iyothee Thass and later, the Mysore area
and Kolar Gold Fields played an important role in Buddhist
educational activities. The conversion to Buddhism of dalit
workers there was a significant event. M. Y. Murugesar, a relative

of Iyothee Thass, began a branch of Sakya Sanga Marikuppam. He, along with E. Guruswamy and A. P. Periyaswamy Pulavar, went to Madras and received Panchasheel. Along with them, G. Appaduraiyar and E. N. Ayyakannu Pulavar took care of the activities of the Sangain Marikuppam.[3] Murugesar, starting from the position of a lowly official in Kolar Gold Fields, rose to become payroll officer and later a contractor for the mines. He built a large hall for the Marikuppam Sanga. In 1908, about a thousand gold mine workers, along with their families, received Panchasheel from an Irish Buddhist monk Visithar. After that the attendance for the weekly meetings in this hall increased manifold. Monks from Sri Lanka, Cambodia, Thailand and Burma preached to workers in this hall. In 1916 a Buddhist Sanga was started in a place called Champion Gold Reeves. Lakshmi Narasu, Periyaswamy Pulavar of Tirupathur, Iyothee Thass's son K. A. Pattabiraman and Sopneswariammal visited this Sanga Both these Sangas were active for more than fifty years.

Marikuppam Sanga ran a library where, palm leaf manuscripts and books on Buddhism and magazines from other countries were preserved. It functioned as a Buddhist centre where occasional talks were held. Full moon days were observed. *Sankaranthi* (winter solstice) day was observed as Buddha's Enlightenment Day and Pongal as a Buddhist festival. Reformist marriages, with the chanting of Buddhist *Dhammapatham* and *Tiriukural* were held in this Sanga. In fact, these were forerunners of Periyar's rationalist marriages. Annapurani and A. Rathanasababathi, who were united in inter-caste marriage in this Sanga later shone as public speakers and writers in the Rationalist movement of Periyar.

The Sanga in the Kolar Gold Fields published books through the printing presses they owned. M. Y. Murugesan who owned M. Y. M. Printing press in Madras and Rajarathinam who owned Siddhartha Printing Press in Kolar Gold Fields brought out new editions of some of Iyothee Thass' books. After the founders of these Sanga passed on, the activities of the Sangas slackened. I. Ulaganathan, son of E. N. Ayyakannu, is now looking after the Buddhist school in Marikuppam and the Buddhists in Kolar Gold Fields.[4]

Periyaswamy Pulavar founded a few Buddhist Sangas in the North Arcot district. He, along with T. N. Hanupanth Upasakar, started a Sanga in Tirupathur. Iyothee Thass's friends, led by P. Lakshmi Narasu, were active in Perambur Buddhist Sanga and its school. The rise and growth of Perambur Buddhist Sanga calls for a separate chapter which is not possible in this essay. Some relatives of Ayyakannu, a teacher in Marikuppam Buddhist School, founded Buddhist Sangas in Natal in South Africa. Iyothee Thass and Krishnaswamy lectured in the Sanga in Yangon.

The earliest seeds of Neo-Buddhism were sown and sprouted among dalits in Madras, Perambur, North Arcot, Kolar Gold Fields and Yangon. But dalits did not benefit fully from the results. It must be remembered that in this period in southern Tamil Nadu, dalits who embraced Protestant Christianity could improve their lot. But among Catholics, upper-caste Christians cornered for themselves any social benefit that converted dalits might get. While Catholic dalits were struggling with upper-caste Christians, the situation of Protestant dalits was different. In Kanyakumari district, dalit Christians joined the Salvation Army which had its headquarters in London. In the Kanyakumari church about 99 percent were dalits. In fact, it was often referred as 'the church of the Pariahs'. It ran the Catherine Booth hospital in Putheri near Nagercoil, which trained many Christians in laboratory technology and nursing. The church also ran schools for Christians. Many from poor families studied in these schools and improved their social status. Some went abroad and grew affluent. Because all the members of the church were dalits, and the head office was in London, these dalits could better their social and financial position. Catholic dalits could not do this because their church was not under their control.

We observed that during the time of Iyothee Thass many dalits in northern Tamil Nadu converted to Buddhism and made progress socially. But they could not match the progress achieved by dalits in Kanyakumari who after conversion were able to get education and jobs. Dalit Buddhists did not get any support from European or Japanese Buddhist institutions. On the other hand, the Buddhists of Sri Lanka received funds and technological benefits from other Buddhist nations. Moreover, many dalits in northern Tamil Nadu who did not convert to Buddhism joined the Non-Brahmin movement, the Dravidian movement and Congress, and gained some political advantage; History cannot be undone. The past is behind us. According to Buddhist logic, everything is changing constantly. And inexorably the consequences of the change will follow.

Many Buddhist dalits of Iyothee Thass's period were active in the field of letters. The best among them was Iyothee Thass himself. He published a number of books through the Buddhist Sanga: *The Adhi Vedam of the Buddha* (1912); *Buddhist Doctrines: Questions and Answers* (1912); *Indhirar Thesa Charithriram* (1931); *VivahaVilakkam* 1926); *Harichandiranin Poykal* (1931). In addition to these, G. Appadurai wrote *Buddharathu Arulamutham* (1950) and Ayyakannu Pulavar, a teacher in Marikuppam Buddhist School wrote songs titled 'Buddha Thoththira Sangeethangal' and set them to music. He also wrote a book of verses titled 'Buddhar Charithira Pa' which is in manuscript form.

The magazine founded by Iyothee Thass, *Thamizhan,* was published from Madras for fourteen years. From 1907 to 1914 (the year of his death) he was the editor. After him, until 1919, his son Pattabiraman published it. From 1919 to 1922 it is not clear who ran it. In 1922, the publication of *Thamizhan* stopped. Later it surfaced and was published from Kolar Gold Fields from 1926 to 1935 with G. Appadurai as the editor.

The anthology of *Thamizhan* magazines, of 1907 to 1914, that Gnana Aloysious has published serves as a veritable archive for that period. The petitions of moderate and extremist factions of the Indian National Congress, news of grama panchayats and Swadeshi demonstrations, the demand for full independence, the efforts of V. O. Chidambaram Pillai to run a shipping company, the riots in Tuticorin and Tirunelveli, the assassination of Collector Ashe by Vanchinathan were all featured in the magazines, with analysis by Iyothee Thass. Ayyakannu Pulavar, a teacher in Marikuppam Buddhist School, as mentioned above, wrote songs and set them to music. The educational work of Christian missionaries, their efforts at conversion, the persistence of caste among Christians and reformative efforts in Hinduism were topics of discussion in the magazine. The impartial and even-handed administration of the British, the activities of the municipalities, and caste-wise representation were also featured. To put it briefly, the Swadeshi movement, British rule, economic, social and political issues and Brahminism were topics often handled by Iyothee Thass in detail from the point of view of dalits.

In the journalistic realm, *Thamizhan* was countering the brahminic thrust of the daily *Swadesamithran* which did not miss any opportunity to denigrate dalits. Iyothee Thass took on that daily at every opportunity. In one issue of *Swadesamithan* (31 Dec 1907) the 'Letters to the Editor' column carried a piece which described how a dalit ran in fear when a Muslim proceeded to hit him with a chappal. The writer attributed his fear to his 'low birth'. In another issue there was a letter which talked about how whites referred to Indians as 'coolies' in Transvaal in South Africa, and Indians were not allowed to get onto trains and in some places not even allowed to walk in the roads. Answering this writer, Iyothee Thass pointed out that in India upper-caste Hindus were treating dalits in a similar manner. Another contemporary writer A. Madhaviah also raised the same question. A reader wrote (17 April 1908) that there should be separate eateries for dalits. Iyothee Thass replied to this reader asking him if he considered dalits a class of animals? He pointed out that the local eating places run by upper castes were unhygienic and even district collectors and judges preferred to eat in Refreshment Rooms and Hotels.

Another reader wrote in *Swadesamithran* (16 April 1908) complaining that caste Hindus are forced to clean their own night soil in prisons and that this is unfair. In response, Iyothee Thass explained the background in *Thamizhan*. During the East India Company period, it was dalit prisoners who were asked to clean the toilets of all prisoners. But when the British government took over the administration, it changed this practice and each prisoner, irrespective of his caste, had to clean his own toilet. He asked why Hindus, who were complacent when dalits cleaned the toilets, were now complaining.

In Bengal, when the pet dog of the Viceroy was bitten by a rabid dog, *Standard* magazine carried a story about the incident. This news was carried in Madras by *Swadesamithran* (12 April 1909) which referred to the animal as a pariah dog. Iyothee Thass pointed this out and said that the publisher of the daily had excess baggage consisting of caste prejudices on his back. *India* magazine behaved in a similar manner while handling caste-related stories. A letter that appeared in *India* (24 April 1908) suggested new school buildings for upper-caste students and separate ones for dalits. Iyothee Thass responded to this and pointed out that money to build schools was not given by brahmins and that even if schools are set up exclusively for dalits, the teachers would be brahmins.

During the times of Iyothee Thass, publications like *Swadesamithran* and *India* run by brahmins worked without any compunction to keeping dalits in their lowly position. They seemed to believe that that was the proper thing to do. They did not hesitate nor were ashamed to propagate Sanathana principles and caste prejudices. Today, in our democratic republic, such prejudices are expressed unobtrusively, shrewdly and euphemistically Upper-caste Hindus

think that shedding caste bias is something they do conde-
scendingly for dalits. They do not try to rectify this age-long
injustice.

To counter the many letters against dalits carried by the
brahminical publications, Iyothee Thass picked up and published articles from other papers that criticized brahmins.
He added his own commentary to such articles and carried
them in *Thamizhan*. For instance, when *Lanka Deepam* magazine featured a story about a brahmin who converted to
Islam, Iyothee Thass expressed his happiness (17 Jan. 1907).
He wrote approvingly about a clash between then Kalai and
Vada Kalai sects in Srirangam during a procession in which
the deity was pushed down. The police had to intervene
and the some of the priests were arrested.

A holy man from Bombay, Venkiah Mahathma, while
staying in Melbourne, embraced and kissed a French girl
who was working as a typist with him. The man was con-
victed and sentenced to six months of hard labour in prison.
Iyothee Thass, tongue in cheek, pointed out that according to
Adhvaitha, it may be all right for the *Paramathma* to forcibly kiss
a *Jeevathma* but according to Australian law it is a criminal act.

In Bengal a retired High Court judge Bapu Sarana Mitra,
started a Hindu Association and was preaching the glories of
ancient Hinduism. Like the Greeks overcoming the Romans
[*sic*] Hindus should overpower the British: everyone should
write only in Devanagari letters: Hindi should be the common
language to unite Hindus. Iyothee Thass took Mitra on and
said that only if he has eternal life, can he think of fulfilling
his dreams.

When Bhupendranath Basu tabled a bill for inter-caste
marriage Iyothee Thass supported it with his characteristic
humour. He wrote that in toddy shops, brothels and coaches
that transport prostitutes, no one is concerned about caste.
After spending the night with women of different castes,
could you be concerned about caste in the morning? So,
he argued, these legislators will not block the bill of Basu.

In another instance when there was a proposal to start a Hindu university he noted that one could not expect the outfit to be without caste biases.

It is evident that among the changes during his period related to politics, religion, society, economics and culture, it was caste prejudice that affected Iyothee Thass deeply. His actions were mainly reactions to caste-related discrimination. This is not the only reason why he went on to propagate Buddhism that was free from such bigotry. One has to acknowledge the role of caste-related atrocities unleashed against dalits in those days. During the British period dalits were eking out livelihoods as butlers, watchmen, traditional medicine-men, in hospitals, in railways, and in the army, and much else, some converted to Christianity, took advantage of the educational and job opportunities extended by the missionaries, and improved their social status. Buddhists like Iyothee Thass were finding their roots in modern life through the Sanga, schools, medical care and journalism. But all this development was possible only in urban areas. In the villages, caste domination, with all its diabolical force, was in operation. Brahminism was trying its best to retain the old Sanathana values. There was none to challenge their attempts except Iyothee Thass. He persistently opposed their efforts. And he chose Dravidian Buddhism as an example of ahimsa of Dravidian Buddhism.

Notes

1 R. Sundaralingam, *Politics of National Awakening in South India. 1882–1891* (Tucson, AZ: University of Arizona Press, 1974).
2 G. Aloysius and K. Perumal, *Revival of Tamil Buddhism. A Historical Survey* (Vellore: Forum for New Society, 1999).
3 G. Appadurai, *Buddharathu Arulamutham* (1950).
4 Samuel.G. John, ed. *Revival of Tamil Buddhism. A Historical Survey* (1998): 158.

References

Aloysius, G. *Religion as Emancipatory Identity: A Buddhist Movement Among the Tamils Under Colonialism.* Chennai: New Age International, 1998.
———. 'Caste in and above History,' *Sociological Bulletin* 48, 1 & 2 (March–Sept. 1998).
———. *Nationalism without a Nation in India.* New Delhi: Oxford University Press.
Appadurai, G. *Buddharathu Arulamutham* (1950)
Narasu, P. Laxmi, 1993, *The Essence of Buddhism,* New Delhi: Asian Educational Services.
Perumal, S. 'Revival of Tamil Buddhism: A Historical Survey'. In *Buddhism in Tamil Nadu, Collected* Papers, Chennai: Institute of Asian Studies, 1998, 529–542, 530–53.
Pulavar, Ayyakannu, *Buddha Thoththira Sangeethangal.*
———. '*Buddhar Charithira Pa*'.
Thass, Iyothee, *The Adhi Vedam of the Buddha* (1912).
———. *Buddhist Doctrines. Questions and Answers* (1912).
———. *Indhirar Thesa Charithriram* (1931).
———. *VivahaVilakkam* (1926).
———. *Harichandiranin Poykal* (1931).

Glossary

Brahmadeva villages	villages granted to brahmins by landlords or regional kings.
cheri	a dalit ghetto.
Kaliyuga	Hindu cosmology says there are four yugas, each decreasing in virtue and righteousness. The last and worst is the age of Kali.
karnam	village official.
kolam	design with rice powder that honours and mimics the cosmic balance on ground outside Hindu houses.
koothu	street drama.
maniam	village revenue official.
munsif	village revenue official.
palayam	unit of land ruled by chieftain in Nayak kingdom.
parai	round percussion instrument, hand held.
pinda	regular offering to ancestors, performed also during funerals.
pongal	rice preparation, literally meaning 'boiling over'; also name of festival.
prasadam	offerings to a deity, sanctified and given to devotees.
tahsildar	revnue official.
thalayari	village headman.
varnashrama	four-fold caste system.

Bibliography

Primary

Chandogya Upanishad, I 12. 1–5.

Sathapathapiramanam II 2.2.6; IV. 3.4.4.

Ambedkar, B. R., and Vasant Moon. *Dr. Babasaheb Ambedkar: Writings and Speeches*, 22 vols. Bombay: Government of Maharashtra, Education Department, for Dr. Babasaheb Ambedkar Source Material Publication Committee, 1982.

Navalar, Arumuga, *Pirapantattiraṭṭu.* Chennai: 1954.

Secondary

Anaimuthu, V. *Periyār Ī. Ve. Rā. cintaṉaikaḷ: patippāciriyar muṉṉurai* (Thoughts of Periyar E.V.R.) Tiruccirāppaḷḷi: Cintaṉaiyāḷar Kaḷakam, 1974.

Ayōttitācar, and G. Aloysius. *Ayōttitācar cintaṉaikaḷ.* Pāḷaiyaṅkōṭṭai: Nāṭṭār Vaḷakkārriyal Āyvu Maiyam, 1999.

Bakhtin, Mikhail Michajlovič, and Hélène Iswolsky. *Rabelais and His World.* Bloomington: Indiana University Press, 1984.

Bakhtin, Mikhail Michajlovič, and Michael Holquist. *The Dialogic Imagination: Four Essays.* Austin: University of Texas Press, 1983.

Bannet, Eve Tavor. *Post-Cultural Theory: Critical Theory after the Marxist Paradigm.* Houndmills: MacMillan Education, 1993.

Baudrillard, Jean. *The Transparency of Evil: Essays on Extreme Phenomena.* London: Verso, 1993.

Civañāṉam, Ma. Po. *Tamiḻanattil piramoliyiṉar.* Chennai: Pulam Veḷiyīṭu, 2009.

Deva, Indra. *Traditional Values and Institutions in Indian Society.* New Delhi.

Dubois, J. A., and Henry K. Beauchamp. *Hindu Manners, Customs and Ceremonies.* New Delhi: Oxford University Press, [1899] 1982.

Freire, Paulo. *Pedagogy of the Oppressed.* London: Penguin, 1973.

Guha, Ranajit, and Gayatri Chakravorty Spivak. *Selected Subaltern Studies.* New Delhi: Oxford University Press, 1988.

Guha, Ranajit. *Elementary Aspects of Peasant Insurgency in Colonial India.* New Delhi: Oxford University Press, 1983.

Holquist, Michael. *Dialogism: Bakhtin and His World.* London: Routledge, 1993.

Karashima, Noboru. *South Indian History and Society: Studies from Inscriptions, A.D. 850–1800.* New Delhi: Oxford University Press, 1984.

Kiruṭṭinaṉ, A. *Kalveṭṭil vāḻviyal.* Ceṉṉai: Maṇivācakar Patippakam, 1991.

Kosambi, D. D., and Es. Ār. Eṉ. Catyā. *Paṇṭaiya intiyā.* Ceṉṉai: Niyū Ceñcuri Puk Havus, 1989.

Krishnaswami, A. *The Tamil Country under Vijayanagar.* Annamalainagar: Annamalai University, 1964.

Kumarakurupara Aṭikaḷ. *Nītineriviḻakkam.* Tarumapuram: Ñāṉacampantam Patippakam, 1943.

Lannoy, Richard. *The Speaking Tree: A Study of Indian Culture and Society.* London: Oxford University Press, 1971.

Mātavaiyā, A. *Patmāvati carittiram: oru Tamiḻ nāṭṭuk katai.* Palghat: T. S. Subramania & Co, 1898.

Nīti veṇpā. Ceṉṉai: Tirunelvēlit Teṉṉintiya Caivacittānta Nūrpatippuk Kaḻakam Limiṭeṭ, 1962.

Parañcōti Muṉivar. *Tiruviḷaiyāṭarpurāṇam.* Ceṉṉai: Vittiyāratnākara Accukkūṭam, 1912.

Śrīmat Pakavatkītai. Tirupparāyttuṛai : Śrīrāmakiruṣṇa Tapōvaṉam, 1974.

Stein, Burton. *Peasant, State, and Society in Medieval South India.* New Delhi: Oxford University Press, 1985.

Tirunāvukkaracu, M. *Maṛaimalaiyaṭikaḷ varalāru.* Tirunelvēli: Tirunelvēlit Teṉṉintiya Caivacittānta Nūrpatippuk Kaḻakam, 1959.

Vanaik, Achin. *The Painful Transition: Bourgeois Democracy in India.* London: Verso, 1990.

Vēṅkaṭacāmi, Mayilai Cīṉi. *Pattoṉpatām nūrrāṇṭil Tamiḻ ilakkiyam: 1800–1900.* Ceṉṉai: Cānti Nūlakam, 1962.

Books by Raj Gauthaman

Ā Kōl Poosalum Perumkarkala Nakarikamum (Cattle Lifting Warfare and Megalithic Civilization). Chennai, Tamizhani, 2009; NCBH, 2nd ed., 2018.

A Madhavaiya 1872–1925. Bengaluru: Kavya, 1995.

A Madhavaiyavin: Tamil Novelkal (Phd Diss.). Chennai: NCBH, 2019.

Aram/Athikaram (Ethics/Power). Coimbatore: Vidiyal, 1997.

Arambakatta Muthalaliyamum Tamil Samooka Matramum (Early Capitalism and Social Changes among Tamils). Chennai: Tamizini, 2009; NCBH, 2nd ed., 2018.

Dalit Panpadu (Dalit Culture), Puducherry, 1993; Chennai: NCBH, 2nd ed., 2019.

Dalit Parvaiyil Tamil Panpadu (Tamil Culture in Dalit Perspective). Madurai: IDEAS, 1994; Chennai: NCBH, 2nd ed., 2019.

Dalitiya Araciyal (Dalit Politics). Chennai: Parisal, 2005; NCBH, 2nd ed., 2019.

Dalitiya Vimarsana Katturai (Critical Essays on Dalits). Nagercoil: Kalachuvadu, 2004.

Empathukalil Tamil Kalacharam (Tamil Culture in the 1980s). Bengaluru: Kavya, 1992; Chennai: NCBH, 2nd ed., 2018.

K. Ayothidasar Ayvukal (Researches of K. Iyothee Thass). Nagercoil: Kalachuvadu, 2004.

Kalachumai (The burden of time; an autobiographical novel). Chennai: Tamizhini, 2003; NCBH, 2nd ed., 2018.

Kalithokai-Paripadal: Oru Vilimbunilai Nokku (*Kalithokai-Paripadal*: A Marginal Approach). Coimbatore: Vidiyal, 2011; Chennai: NCBH, 2nd ed., 2020.

Kanmoodi Vazhakkamellam Manmoodippoha, C. Ramalingam, 1823–1874, Chennai: Tamizhini, 2001; NCBH, 2nd ed., 2018.

Londonil Siluvai Raj (Siluvai Raj in London). Chennai: Tamizhini, 2005; NCBH, 2nd ed., 2018.

Pathirtrupathu Aingurunooru Sila Avathanippukal (Some Observations). Chennai: Tamizhini, 2010; NCBH, 2nd ed., 2018.

Pattum Thokaiyum Tholkappiamum, Tamil Samooka Uruvakamum (Ten Idylls and Eight Anthologies, *Tolkappiyam* and Social Formation). Chennai: 2006; NCBH, 2nd ed., 2018.

Pazhanthamizh Ahaval Padalkalil Parimatrankal. Chennai: NCBH, 2019.

Poi + Abatham > Unmai (False + Absurdity > Truth). Coimbatore: Vilimbu Trust Publication, 1995; Chennai: NCBH, 2nd ed., 2018.

Pudumaippithan Ennum Bhramma Rakshus. Chennai: Tamizhani, 2000; NCBH, 2nd ed., 2018.

Siluvai Raj Charithram (The history of Siluvai Raj; an autobiographical novel). Chennai: Tamizhini, 2002; NCBH, 2nd ed., 2019.

Sundara Ramasamy: Karuthum Kalaiyum. Chennai: NCBH, 2019.

Tamil Samookathil Aramum Artralum (ethics and power in Tamil society). Coimbatore: 2008; Chennai, NCBH, 2nd ed., 2018.

Translations by Raj Gauthaman

Anbu Enum Kalai: Erich Fromm (*The Art of Loving* by Erich Fromm, 1956). Chennai: NCBH, 2019.

Kathaikkaruvoolam (*Kathakosa—Samana Samaya Kathaikal* by C. H. Thani). Coimbatore: Vidiyal, 2011; Chennai: NCBH, 2020.

Kilikkathaikal Ezhupathu (Śukasaptati, *Seventy Tales of the Parrot*). Chennai: Tamizhani, 2011; Nagercoil, Kalachuvadu, 2nd ed., 2017.

Manavalamaana Samuthaayam: Erich Fromn (*The Sane Society* by Erich Fromm, 1955). Nagercoil: *Kalachuvadu, 2014.*

Palatra PenpalL Germain Greer (*The Female Eunuch* by Germaine Greer). Coimbatore: Vidiyal, 2011; Chennai: NCBH, 2nd ed., 2020.

Penniyam: Varalarum Kotpatukalum: Sarah Gamble, Toril Moi (*Feminism: History of Theories*). Coimbatore: Vidiyal, 2011; Chennai: NCBH, 2nd ed., 2018.

Uyirinankalin Thotram: Charles Darwin (*Origin of Species through Natural Selection* by Charles Darwin). Coimbatore: Vidiyal, 2010; Chennai: NCBH, 2nd ed., 2019.

Vilimbunilai Makkalin Porattangal (Ranajit Guha, Susie Tharu and Tejaswini Niranjana). Nagercoil: Kalachuvadu, 2016.

About the Author and the Translator

Raj Gauthaman (b. 1950, Virudhnagar) is a leading Tamil intellectual who was part of a core group of mainly dalit writers and thinkers in the 1990s who were behind the influential little magazine, *Nirapirigai*. He has authored twenty research works that analyse the development of Tamil culture from ancient to modern periods with a focus on subaltern dalit perspectives. He retired as Head of the Tamil Department at the Kanchi Mamunivar Centre for Postgraduate Studies in Puducherry.

S. Theodore Baskaran (b. 1940), writes in both Tamil and English. His book *The Message Bearers* (1981) is a standard reference work on the freedom struggle in South India. His book *The Eye of the Serpent: An Introduction to Tamil Cinema* (1996) won the Swarna Kamal award from the President of India. He has translated Ullas Kanth, *The Way of the Tiger* (2004) and Job Thomas, *The Chola Bronzes* (2019) into Tamil.

Index